The Ultimate Zoom Cookbook

Over 100 recipes to enhance and engage
communication with Zoom

Patrick Kelley

The Ultimate Zoom Cookbook

Group Product Manager: Aaron Tanna

Publishing Product Manager: Uzma Sheerin

Book Project Manager: Prajakta Naik

Senior Editor: Kinnari Chohan

Technical Editor: Jubit Pincy

Copy Editor: Safis Editing

Proofreader: Kinnari Chohan

Indexer: Pratik Shirodkar

Production Designer: Prafulla Nikalje

DevRel Marketing Coordinator: Deepak Kumar and Mayank Singh

First published: June 2024

Production reference: 1240524

Published by Packt Publishing Ltd.

Grosvenor House

11 St Paul's Square

Birmingham

B3 1RB, UK

ISBN 978-1-80461-699-4

www.packtpub.com

To my family, who have been patient enough to endure many nights and weekends without me as I stared at a screen, wishing I knew how to write.

– Patrick Kelley

Contributors

About the author

Patrick Kelley, better known as the *Tattooed Nerd*, is a Distinguished Architect at Zoom. As Chief Technical Evangelist in the industry, he leads sales and competitive enablement efforts worldwide, is a content creator on platforms like YouTube and LinkedIn, and has been named in the Top 50 UCaaS influencers in the world. With over 25 years in the industry, he has worked for prestigious companies like ESPN, Citrix, and Microsoft. As an awarded public speaker, he has presented at conferences like Microsoft Ignite and Zoomtopia, leading thought leadership sessions as well as deep technical roundtables in the collaboration and communication industry.

About the reviewer

Patrick Nowicki is an IT industry veteran with over 25 years in the collaboration space. Patrick currently works in the competitive market strategy team at Zoom providing invaluable advice to Zoom's sales, product development, and partners, leveraging his extensive background which includes experience with industry leaders such as Cisco, Microsoft, RingCentral, and Zoom. Before Zoom, Patrick spent more than 20 years as a channel partner, consulting with customers and developing services in the collaboration technology space.

Table of Contents

3

Managing Zoom Meetings   95

4

Zoom Phone   121

7

AI Companion   217

8

Security and Privacy   251

9

Advanced Tips and Tricks   271

Appendix A   313

Appendix B   321

Index   329

Other Books You May Enjoy   336

Preface

Welcome to the era of **Zoom**—a realm where geographical boundaries blur and connectivity transcends the limitations of physical distance. In this digital epoch, the way we communicate, collaborate, and connect has undergone a seismic shift, and at the heart of this transformation lies Zoom.

This book is not just a manual on how to navigate the intricacies of Zoom's interface or a technical guide to mastering its features. Instead, it's a testament to the profound impact Zoom has had on our lives, both personally and professionally. It delves into the nuances of virtual communication, explores the challenges and triumphs of remote work, and examines the importance of communication and collaboration with other co-workers, colleagues, family, friends, and customers.

We will not only dive into many of the Zoom features that can be utilized but also cover the use cases of why it should be used, giving real-world examples of the importance of the tool as well as when it should or can be utilized.

Through the pages of this book, we'll delve into the wealth of modalities that can be used within Zoom. Zoom isn't just a video conferencing tool anymore. It's a complete platform driven by simple to advanced feature sets. Of course, audio and video are paramount to Zoom's success, but we will also uncover many other areas, including webinars, Zoom Phone, app integration, and even AI. We'll uncover the intricacies of virtual etiquette, unravel the secrets of effective virtual collaboration, and perhaps gain a deeper understanding of the human need for connection in an increasingly digitized world. Zoom's goal is to bring limitless human connection and will cover all the ways that can transpire inside of this wonderful application.

In essence, this book is a tribute to the resilience of the human spirit, the ingenuity of technological innovation, and the enduring power of human connection. Whether you're a seasoned Zoom veteran or a newcomer to the world of virtual communication, I invite you to embark on this journey with an open mind and a curiosity for the boundless possibilities that lie ahead. Zoom is a powerful tool and when harnessed correctly can bring great efficiency and productivity to any user.

So, let us venture forth into the digital realm, where the boundaries between virtual and reality blur, and where the only limit is our imagination. Welcome to the Zoom era—a world of infinite connections, awaiting exploration.

Top of Form

Who this book is for

The target audience of this book is quite diverse, reflecting the wide range of individuals and organizations that use the platform. Zoom started as an enterprise-specific application, but its ease of use and simple design caused this tool to be easily adopted by consumers all over the globe:

- **Business professionals**: This group includes corporate executives, managers, team leaders, and employees who rely on Zoom for remote meetings, presentations, and collaboration. They may seek guidance on optimizing their use of Zoom for productivity and effectiveness in a virtual work environment.

- **Educators and students**: With the rise of online learning, teachers, professors, and students may benefit from this book as it explores best practices for virtual classrooms, engaging remote students, and utilizing Zoom for lectures, discussions, and group projects.

- **Freelancers and remote workers**: Individuals who work independently or remotely, such as freelancers, consultants, and digital nomads, may find value in learning how to leverage Zoom for client meetings, networking, and maintaining professional connections from anywhere in the world.

- **Nonprofit organizations and community groups**: Charities, nonprofits, and community organizations often rely on Zoom for virtual events, fundraising, and volunteer coordination. This book offers insights into using Zoom for outreach, collaboration, and building virtual communities.

- **Healthcare professionals**: Telemedicine has become increasingly prevalent, especially considering public health crises. Healthcare providers, therapists, counselors, and medical administrators may seek guidance on using Zoom for virtual patient consultations, therapy sessions, and staff meetings while maintaining patient confidentiality and adhering to regulatory requirements.

- **Families and social groups**: In an era of social distancing, families, friends, and social clubs have turned to Zoom for virtual gatherings, celebrations, and game nights. This book provides tips for making virtual interactions more engaging, fun, and meaningful.

- **Tech enthusiasts and innovators**: Those interested in the intersection of technology and society may find value in this book that explores emerging trends in virtual communication and collaboration technologies.

From simple and effective virtual interactions to advanced features such as **artificial intelligence** (**AI**) in the realm of communication and collaboration, this Zoom cookbook targets the beginner to the advanced user.

What this book covers

Chapter 1, Understanding the Basics of Zoom, introduces the basic UCaaS functionality, outlining the differences between collaboration (email, chat, file sharing) and real-time communication (audio, video, content sharing). You will explore the basic functions of Zoom and the overall interface and cover tips for setting up meetings, inviting participants, and managing Zoom settings.

Chapter 2, Content Sharing and Collaboration, introduces content sharing during 1:1 and meetings. Examples of what content can be shared (files, screens, programs, & whiteboards) will be given, and the different ways content can be shared with other users and meeting attendees will be described. You will be given walk-throughs and screenshots of exactly how to share content before, during, and after a meeting.

Chapter 3, Managing Zoom Meetings, will teach you about the best practices for conducting proper Zoom meetings. You will understand how to manage time effectively during virtual meetings and learn how to use effective collaboration tools such as chat, annotations, and reactions. You will be shown proper strategies for maintaining the focus of content during a meeting, and you will learn how to use effective meeting controls.

Chapter 4, Zoom Phone, introduces Zoom Phone, a comprehensive cloud-based communication solution that integrates seamlessly with the Zoom platform, offering businesses a unified communications experience. You will be shown how users can make and receive calls, send text messages, and hold video meetings all from a single application, enhancing productivity and collaboration within organizations.

Chapter 5, Zoom Team Chat, introduces Team Chat, a robust collaboration tool designed to streamline communication and foster teamwork within organizations. With features tailored for group messaging, file sharing, and integration with other Zoom services, Zoom Team Chat offers a comprehensive chat solution for modern workplace communication needs.

Chapter 6, Zoom Webinars, shows you how to create and manage both small- and large-scale webinars, implementing strategies for increased user engagement. This chapter also dives deep into increasing attendee interactions with tools such as Polls/Quizzes, Q&A, and Chat.

Chapter 7, AI Companion, shows you how to implement AI into your communication and collaboration workflows. This chapter provides insights into how to streamline productivity and enhance efficiency using Zoom's own tool, AI Companion, with modalities such as Chat, email, whiteboards, and even Zoom Phone.

Chapter 8, Security and Privacy, shows you how to implement best practice security and privacy tools in Zoom with specific walk-throughs regarding meetings and webinars. It dives deep into authentication, encryption, and attendee controls for safer Zoom interactions.

Chapter 9, Advanced Tips and Tricks, will help you become a Zoom master as we dive deep into the Zoom client's advanced features and learn how to use them in your everyday workflows. You will learn how to implement AI with your recordings or even implement live streaming on platforms such as YouTube.

To get the most out of this book

Before we start, let's go over the supported scenarios for using the Zoom client. Make sure your device meets the minimum requirements for the operating system, processor, web browser, and bandwidth before installing the Zoom client.

For the latest technical requirements, visit Zoom's system requirements page: Zoom System Requirements at `https://support.zoom.com/hc/en/article?id=zm_kb&sysparm_article=KB0060748`.

Conventions used

There are a few text conventions used throughout this book:

Bold: Indicates a new term, an important word, or words that you see onscreen. For example, words in menus or dialog boxes appear in the text like this. Here is an example: "Click on the profile icon in the top-right corner and choose the **Check for Updates** option."

> **Tips or important notes**
> Appear like this.

Sections

In this book, you will find several headings that appear frequently (*Getting ready*, *How to do it...*, and *There's more...*).

To give clear instructions on how to complete a recipe, use these sections as follows:

Getting ready

This section tells you what to expect in the recipe and describes how to set up any software or any preliminary settings required for the recipe.

How to do it...

This section contains the steps required to follow the recipe.

There's more...

This section consists of additional information about the recipe in order to make you more knowledgeable about the recipe.

Get in touch

Feedback from our readers is always welcome.

General feedback: If you have questions about any aspect of this book, mention the book title in the subject of your message and email us at customercare@packtpub.com.

Errata: Although we have taken every care to ensure the accuracy of our content, mistakes do happen. If you have found a mistake in this book, we would be grateful if you would report this to us. Please visit www.packtpub.com/support/errata, select your book, click on the Errata Submission Form link, and enter the details.

Piracy: If you come across any illegal copies of our works in any form on the Internet, we would be grateful if you would provide us with the location address or website name. Please contact us at copyright@packt.com with a link to the material.

If you are interested in becoming an author: If there is a topic that you have expertise in and you are interested in either writing or contributing to a book, please visit authors.packtpub.com.

Share your thoughts

Once you've read *The Ultimate Zoom Cookbook*, we'd love to hear your thoughts! Scan the QR code below to go straight to the Amazon review page for this book and share your feedback.

https://packt.link/r/1804616990

Your review is important to us and the tech community and will help us make sure we're delivering excellent quality content.

Download a free PDF copy of this book

Thanks for purchasing this book!

Do you like to read on the go but are unable to carry your print books everywhere?

Is your eBook purchase not compatible with the device of your choice?

Don't worry, now with every Packt book you get a DRM-free PDF version of that book at no cost.

Read anywhere, any place, on any device. Search, copy, and paste code from your favorite technical books directly into your application.

The perks don't stop there, you can get exclusive access to discounts, newsletters, and great free content in your inbox daily

Follow these simple steps to get the benefits:

1. Scan the QR code or visit the link below

https://packt.link/free-ebook/9781804616994

2. Submit your proof of purchase
3. That's it! We'll send your free PDF and other benefits to your email directly

1
Understanding the Basics of Zoom

Zoom is a very powerful communication and collaboration platform that allows for a multitude of ways to interact with people. Using simple text with things such as email and chat to fully immersive modalities such as audio, video, and content sharing, Zoom can be as simple or as advanced as you want. We are going introduce the basics of **Unified Communications/Collaboration as a Service (UCaaS)** functionality and define the various modalities that can be used. We will be outlining the differences between collaboration (email, chat, file sharing, whiteboard, and so on) and real-time communication (audio, video, content sharing, phone, and so on). Then, you will learn how to download, install, and log in to Zoom. Next, we will explore the basic functions of Zoom and the overall interface, such as joining and creating meetings, setting up email and calendar, as well as creating contacts. Finally, we will explore how to invite participants, manage meeting settings, and use some of the advanced functions inside the Zoom client.

In this chapter, we're going to cover the following main recipes:

- Downloading the Zoom client
- Logging in to Zoom
- Joining a Zoom meeting
- Setting up your email and calendar
- Creating contacts
- Setting up a Zoom meeting

Technical requirements

Before we begin, let's review a few of the supported scenarios for the Zoom client. You will need to have the minimum supported operating system, processor, web browser, and bandwidth requirements before you can install the Zoom client.

To get up-to-date technical requirements, be sure to visit Zoom's system requirements page: `https://support.zoom.com/hc/en/article?id=zm_kb&sysparm_article=KB0060748`.

Supported operating systems

Desktop operating systems:

- macOS X with macOS X (10.10) or later
- Windows 11
- Windows 10
- Windows 8 or 8.1
- Windows 7
- ChromeOS
- Ubuntu 12.04 or higher
- Mint 17.1 or higher
- Red Hat Enterprise Linux 6.4 or higher
- Oracle Linux 6.4 or higher
- CentOS 6.4 or higher
- Fedora 21 or higher
- openSUSE 13.2 or higher
- ArchLinux (64-bit only)

Mobile operating systems:

- iOS 8.0* or later
- iPhone 4 or later, iPad Pro, iPad Mini, iPad 2 or later, iPod Touch 4th generation, iPhone 3GS (no front-facing camera)
- iPadOS 13 or later
- Android 5.0x or later

Processor requirements

Desktop devices:

- Single-core 1 GHz or higher
- (Recommended) Dual-core 2 GHz or higher (Intel i3/i5/i7 or AMD equivalent)

Mobile devices:

- Any 1 GHz single-core processor or better (non-Intel)

Supported web browsers

Desktop:

- **Chrome**: Within two versions of the current version
- **Firefox**: Within two versions of the current version
- **Edge**: Within two versions of the current version
- **Safari**: Within two versions of the current version

Mobile:

- **Safari**: Within 2 versions of the current version
- **Chrome**: Within 2 versions of the current version

For instance, if the current version of Chrome on mobile is 111, then the Zoom web app is supported on versions 109, 110, and 111. As new versions are released, the minimum version will also be followed behind by two versions.

> **Note**
>
> These are the web browsers that Zoom officially supports. While the Zoom web app and web client might function in other browsers, note that those browsers aren't officially endorsed. Their compatibility and functionality may vary. Additionally, while older versions of web browsers may still function, it's advisable to stick to two versions of the current one for optimal performance.

Downloading the Zoom client

In this recipe, you will learn where to download the Zoom client, depending on what operating system and hardware you want to use. Zoom combines video and audio conferencing, online meetings, whiteboards, telephony, and chat messaging into one easy-to-use application. Zoom offers video, audio, screen, content sharing, phone and even conferencing room capabilities from one simple client.

How to do it...

To download the Zoom desktop client, do the following:

1. In your internet browser, enter `https://zoom.us/`.

2. At the top of the main page, click the **Resources** tab:

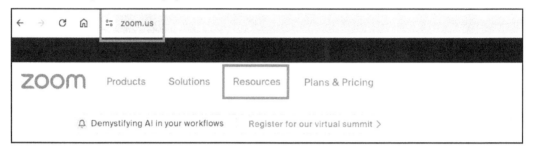

Figure 1.1: Resources tab

3. Then, click **Download Center**:

Figure 1.2: Download Center link

4. Under **Zoom Desktop Client**, click the **Download** button.

> **Note**
> If you are on a Mac with an Apple silicon chip, use the install URL beneath the **Download** button.

Depending on which browser you are using, the Zoom installer (`ZoomInstaller.exe` for Windows, `zoomusInstallerFull.pkg` for macOS, or the 32-bit/64-bit Linux installer) will automatically start downloading the Zoom desktop client:

Zoom Desktop Client

Phone, Meetings, Chat, Whiteboard and more for your desktop.

The web browser client will download automatically when you start or join your first Zoom meeting, and is also available for manual download here.

 Version 5.17.2 (28415)

Or, for Macs with Apple Silicon chips, click here to download

Figure 1.3: Zoom Download button

1. Complete the installation process. This should begin immediately after downloading, but if not, browse to where you downloaded the client and *double-click* on your install package.

> **Note**
>
> After the Zoom desktop client installation is complete, a Zoom icon will appear on your desktop. *Double-click* the Zoom desktop icon to begin using Zoom.

iOS

To download the Zoom mobile app for Apple iOS:

1. Open the **App Store** app from your iPhone or iPad.
2. Enter Zoom in the search box.
3. Once your search results appear, tap **Zoom - One Platform to Connect**. (**Note**: Do not choose **Zoom for Intune** unless directed so by your IT department.)
4. Tap **Get**.
5. Zoom will start to download on your iOS device.
6. (**Note**: When the Zoom mobile app finishes the installation, the Zoom app icon will appear on your **Home** screen.)
7. After you finish downloading the Zoom mobile app, you can access and begin using Zoom by the following methods:

    - If you stayed on Zoom's **App Store** page, tap **OPEN**.

    - If you exited the App Store, tap the Zoom mobile app icon on your Home screen.

Android

To download the Zoom mobile app for Android, do the following:

1. Tap the **Google Play** icon.

2. At the bottom of your screen, tap **Apps**.

3. At the top right of your screen, tap the **Search** icon.

4. Enter Zoom in the search box.

5. Once your search results appear, tap **Zoom - One Platform to Connect**.

6. Tap the **Install** button.

7. Tap **Accept** to confirm the installation.

8. Zoom will start to download on your Android device.

9. (**Note**: When the Zoom mobile app finishes the installation, the Zoom app icon will appear on your Home screen.)

10. After you finish downloading the Zoom mobile app, you can access and begin using Zoom by the following methods:

    - If you stayed on Zoom's Google Play page, tap **Open**.

    - If you exited Google Play, tap the Zoom mobile app icon on your Home screen.

Logging in to Zoom

To first log in to Zoom, you will need to create either a free or paid Zoom account. There are several levels of Zoom accounts, from Basic (Free) to Enterprise (which is a company-level account). To see which account level fits your requirements, please review the **Plans & Pricing** page from Zoom at the following websites:

- **Business**: https://Zoom.us/pricing

- **Personal**: https://Zoom.us/pricing#personal

Once you have determined which account suits your needs, proceed to the following login steps.

How to do it...

Personal account

1. Launch the Zoom client. By default, Zoom creates an icon on the desktop after successful installation. If you installed Zoom in a custom location, launch the Zoom client from there.

    Once the client has launched, you will see several choices for sign-in. Choose the sign-in method that would be best for you (see *Figure 1.4*):

*   **SSO** – Single sign-on. This choice is primarily for Business/Enterprise accounts that have accounts already established from within your IT department. The username and password would be most likely provided by your IT department.

    i.   **Apple** – If you have an Apple ID, you can use it to create your personal Zoom account.

    ii. **Google** – You can also use your Google and Gmail accounts to create your Zoom account.

    iii. **Facebook** – Your Facebook ID also works to create a personal Zoom account.

    If you don't have any of the aforementioned, please move to *step 3* to set up your account directly with Zoom:

Figure 1.4: Sign-in options

2. For users wanting to create a personal account without signing in using any of the methods in *step 1*, click the **Sign Up** option at the bottom right of the login page:

Figure 1.5: Sign Up link

i. You must verify your age on the next page. Type in your birth year and click **Continue**:

Figure 1.6: Age verification

ii. Enter the email address you would like to use to log on to Zoom:

Figure 1.7: Email address

iii. Zoom will generate a verification code and send it to your email account. Enter the code generated in Zoom:

Figure 1.8: Code verification

iv. Create your Zoom account by typing in the following fields:

- **First Name**
- **Last Name**
- **Password**

(**Note**: If you are an educator creating accounts on behalf of students, please check the **For Educators** box.) With this, you're done! You will now be logged in to Zoom with your new account:

Figure 1.9: Creating an account

Business account

If you're using a Business- or Enterprise-level account, it's probable that your IT administrator has already set up and established your account before your login attempt. This information likely has been communicated to you via email. There are two main methods for logging in to a Business account:

1. Company email and password
2. **SSO**

Use the method that has been directed by your IT department. If you have questions as to which method your company uses, contact your help desk.

> **Note**
> Visit *Appendix B* to familiarize yourself with some of the functions of the Zoom client.

Joining a Zoom meeting

In this recipe, we will learn how to join a Zoom meeting. There are three basic ways to join a Zoom meeting. The first is to manually enter a meeting ID; this is the least commonly used method. The second is to click on the **Join** button from your Zoom, Google, or Outlook calendar; this is probably the most common method. The third method is to click the **Join Zoom Meeting** URL that came with your meeting invitation. We will walk through all three methods as there are multiple ways to join a Zoom meeting.

Typically, when you are invited to a Zoom meeting you will be sent a calendar invite in your email or Zoom **Team Chat**. This has the meeting ID and passcode, as well as the **Join Zoom Meeting** link.

How to do it...

Method 1 (meeting ID)

1. Open the Zoom desktop client.

2. Navigate to the Home screen by clicking **Home** at the top of the navigation bar you learned about in the previous recipe.

3. Click the **Join** button:

Figure 1.10: Join button

4. Enter the *meeting ID*. This is the 9-11 digit unique number that was sent to you when you were invited to a Zoom meeting:

Join Meeting

Meeting ID or personal link name

Zoom Account

◯ Don't connect to audio
◯ Turn off my video

Cancel   Join

Figure 1.11: Meeting ID

5. By default, your account name will be in the **Your Name** section, but you can edit it here as well. When you join the Zoom meeting, this is the name that will be displayed to other people in the meeting.

6. Select if you would like to connect audio or video.

7. Click **Join**.

8. You will be prompted for a passcode. Enter the six-digit passcode that was sent in your meeting invite, then click **OK**.

9. That's it! You'll be joined to your Zoom meeting.

Method 2 (joining from the calendar)

1. Open the Zoom desktop application.

    Navigate to the right side of Zoom. Here, you will see the Calendar Panel. Any meetings that you were invited to for the day will appear here, populated with all users invited and the Zoom meeting information.

2. Click the **Join** button to launch your Zoom meeting:

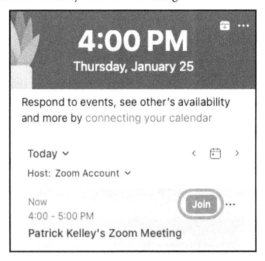

Figure 1.12: Joining a Zoom meeting

> **Note**
>
> When joining a meeting from a calendar invite, you will not need to enter the meeting ID or passcode. These are embedded in the meeting invite and aren't required to be entered manually as in *method 1*.

Method 3 (joining from a browser link)

1. Launch your email application (Outlook or Gmail/Google Mail).

2. Navigate to the email that was sent to you for the meeting invitation.

3. In the body of the email, you will see **Join Zoom Meeting**:

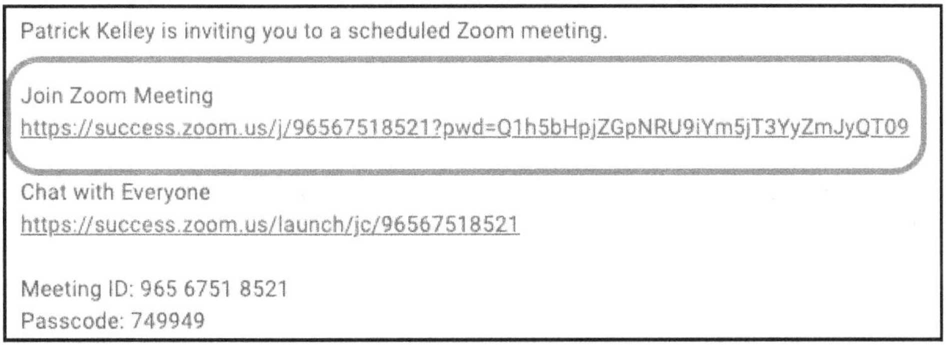

Patrick Kelley is inviting you to a scheduled Zoom meeting.

Join Zoom Meeting
https://success.zoom.us/j/96567518521?pwd=Q1h5bHpjZGpNRU9iYm5jT3YyZmJyQT09

Chat with Everyone
https://success.zoom.us/launch/jc/96567518521

Meeting ID: 965 6751 8521
Passcode: 749949

Figure 1.13: Join Zoom Meeting

4. Click on the hyperlink beneath **Join Zoom Meeting**, as highlighted in the previous figure. Zoom will launch your meeting!

> **Note**
>
> Just as with *method 2*, the meeting ID and passcode are embedded in the meeting link and therefore will not need to be entered manually.

Setting up your email and calendar

Zoom can be configured as your email and calendar client with either Microsoft Outlook or Google Mail. This has many advantages. Users can be more efficient and productive as Zoom can now be used to read, reply, and forward emails just like your current email provider. We can also synchronize the Zoom calendar with either Outlook or Google. You will then be able to see not only all your Zoom meetings but any meeting in your calendar. This is a great time saver because as a user, you will no longer need to switch between Zoom and your email client. This will also help you to use Zoom as your primary email and calendar client.

Getting ready

In order to utilize the **Zoom Mail** client feature, you will have to be utilizing either Microsoft or Google as your primary email and calendar client before setting up the **Zoom Mail & Calendar** service.

How to do it...

1. Launch your Zoom desktop client. Navigate to your **Mail** icon located at the top navigation bar and click on your email/calendar provider (**Google** or **Microsoft**).

2. You will be prompted to log in to your email account. Enter your email address and password and then click **Continue**.

    The Zoom **Admin** portal will open and prompt you with a **Select a Service** option. Pick which provider you use.

> **Note**
>
> In this example, we will be using Google, but the steps are the same for Office 365. On rare occasions, some businesses might still have Exchange deployed on-premises. This cookbook is outside the scope of that situation. Contact your IT department for appropriate steps to connect Zoom and Microsoft Exchange.

3. In this example, we will choose **Google**. We will choose all settings for **Read and Write**. This will give Zoom permission to **Mail**, **Calendar**, **Contacts**, and **Drive**:

> **Note**
>
> We will dive deeper into Google Drive in the *How to use Zoom apps* recipe, but for now, you can enable this feature if you use the Google productivity suite and want to share files directly from Zoom. If you chose Office 365 as your email provider, we will also cover OneDrive and Zoom integration in the aforementioned recipe.

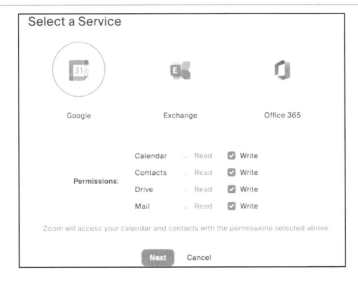

Figure 1.14: Select a Service

4. Next, click **Select All** to allow Zoom to access your Google account, then click **Continue**:

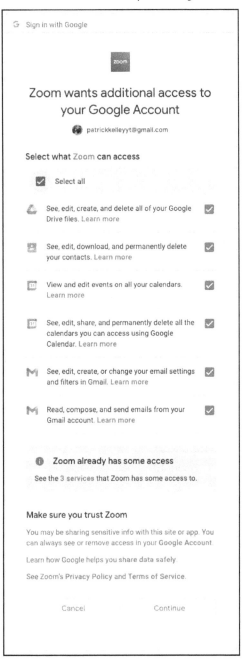

Figure 1.15: Google account access

5. You've now properly configured Zoom to work with your email and calendar.

6. Click on the **Mail** or **Calendar** icon in your Zoom client. You should now be able to view all your email and calendar items from your provider.

Congratulations!

Creating contacts

Contacts are your way of interacting with people you contribute with frequently. Ways to communicate with your contacts are chat, audio, and video. If you have a Zoom Phone license, you will also be able to utilize SMS and PSTN calling with contacts. Your Zoom **Contacts** directory contains all users on the same account. For example, if you are a business and have 500 Zoom users, you will see all of them in the **Contacts** directory. But if you're a small business or a single user, you will have to add personal contacts. If you have configured Zoom to integrate with Office 365 or Google, your contacts will be synchronized to Zoom and be available to communicate and collaborate with. In this recipe, you will learn how to create contacts and how to interact with them.

How to do it...

1. Sign in to the Zoom desktop client.

2. Click the **Contacts** tab on your top navigation bar.

3. At the top left of the screen, you will see a + icon. Click it to add a contact.

4. Two choices will be displayed:

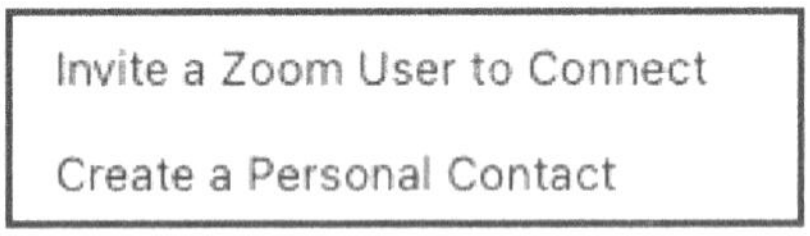

Invite a Zoom User to Connect

Create a Personal Contact

Figure 1.16: Zoom Contacts

> **Note**
> - If you know your contact uses Zoom, choose **Invite a Zoom User to Connect**.
> - If you are adding a contact that isn't on Zoom, choose **Create a Personal Contact**.
> - If you are using Google Mail, an option to add a Google contact will appear.
> - If you are using Outlook, an option to add an Outlook contact will appear.

5. To invite a Zoom user, enter their email address, then click **Invite**:

Figure 1.17: Invite to Zoom

6.   An invite will be sent to your contact via Zoom.

7.   If you choose **Create a Personal Contact**, you will be prompted to enter their information:

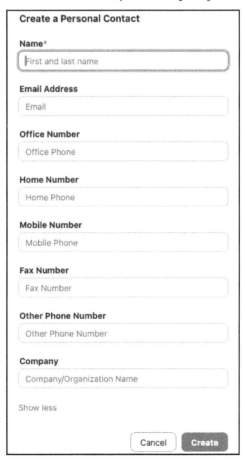

Figure 1.18: Personal contact information

8. After adding a personal contact, you will be able to communicate with them via SMS and phone if you have a Zoom Phone license. You can also invite them to Zoom as a contact. They will receive an invite to join Zoom via email, which opens other avenues of communication such as **Chat and Meet** if they accept:

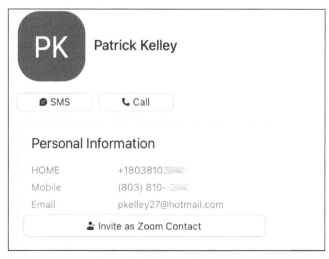

Figure 1.19: Personal contact

9. After your contact accepts your Zoom invitation, you can then see additional modalities to communicate and collaborate with them:

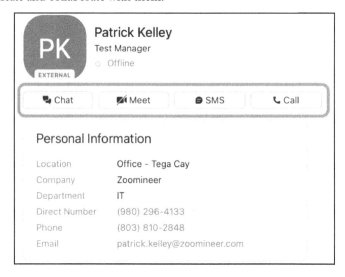

Figure 1.20: Contact modalities

Your Zoom contact, as opposed to a personal contact, will contain more pertinent information such as **Presence** (that is, **Online**, **Busy**, **Away**, **Out of Office**, **Available**), **Location**, **Department**, and **Company**:

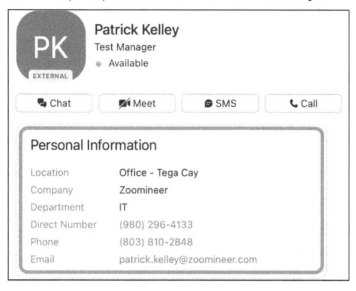

Figure 1.21: Contact information

Any contact you deem more important than others or whom you communicate with more often can be *starred*. This prioritizes the contact into your starred list for easier access. To star a contact, click the star icon next to their name:

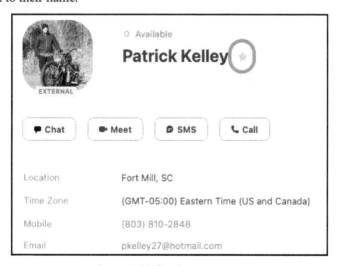

Figure 1.22: Starring a contact

You're done. You now know how to add contacts in Zoom!

Setting up a Zoom meeting

With Zoom, you can set up multiple ways to interact with both internal and external contacts, partners, customers, and vendors. Three different modalities can be used for this:

- Use the Zoom client to email your contact
- Use **Team Chat** to interact via chat
- Use video and audio for a fully immersive meeting

We will walk through all these steps individually.

How to do it...

Emailing a Zoom contact

1. Choose **Mail** at the top of your navigation bar in the Zoom client.

2. Once your mail client opens, you will see a blue pencil icon in the top-right area:

> **Note**
> In this example, we have configured our Zoom client to use Office 365, therefore it says **Microsoft**. If you had chosen Gmail as your email client, this area would say **Google**.

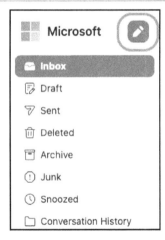

Figure 1.23: Composing an email

3. Click on the blue pencil icon to compose an email.

4.   A **New Mail** window will open:

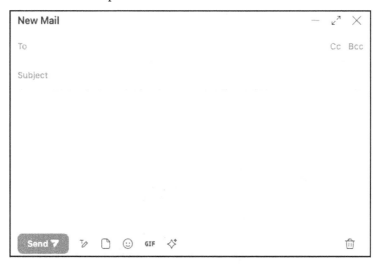

Figure 1.24: Email compose window

5.   Now, compose your email by entering the email address of your intended audience. This can be one or hundreds of addresses.

6.   Enter anyone you want CC:ed (carbon copy) or Bcc:ed (blind carbon copy).

7.   Enter your subject line and compose the email. Include any relevant attachments (documents, pictures, files) if needed, and click the **Send** button when done:

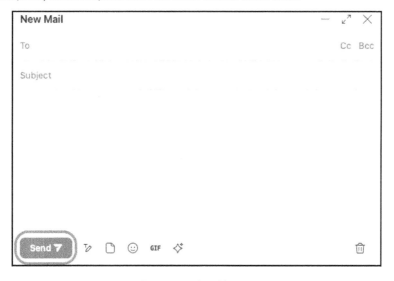

Figure 1.25: Send button

And you're done! Email composition is complete.

Chatting with another Zoom user

1. Click the **Team Chat** icon at the top of the navigation bar.

2. The Zoom **Team Chat** client will open.

3. To compose a chat, click the blue + icon:

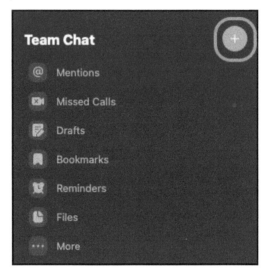

Figure 1.26: Team Chat compose

4. When you click on the + icon, a **New** window will hover open. Click the **Chat** option:

Figure 1.27: Starting a new chat

5. A new **Team Chat** compose window will open. In the **To:** section, enter the person or contact you would like to chat with. This could be a contact you've already added or the email address of the user. In the **Message…** section, enter what you want to chat with the person about:

Figure 1.28: Team Chat compose window

> **Note**
>
> If the user you're attempting to chat with is already on Zoom, they will receive your **Team Chat** message and can reply back. If the user you are attempting to chat with is not on Zoom, they will receive an email with an invitation to join your **Team Chat** channel. Once they have accepted your invitation, they will be able to reply to your chat request.

6. You can also click on **Contacts** in your top navigation bar and choose any contact that has been added. Once you click on the person, their information will appear with a choice to use **Chat**. You can start a new conversation here as well as continue any past **Team Chat** conversations:

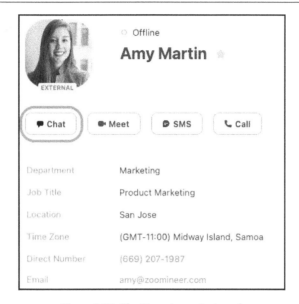

Figure 1.29: Chatting via contact card

7.   That's it! You now know how to start a chat.

Meeting with a user/contact

There are several methods to meet with a user using audio and video from Zoom. Let's review the most common ways to start a Zoom meeting with someone 1:1.

Inviting from the Home screen

1.   Click on the **Home** icon at the top of your navigation bar.

2.   Click the orange **New Meeting** button.

3.   The Zoom **Meeting** client will launch in a new window.

4.   At the bottom, you will see a **Participants** icon with a 1. This is because you are the only one in the meeting.

5.   To invite other participants, click the up caret (^) and choose **Invite…**:

Figure 1.30: Inviting meeting participants

6. After you click **Invite...**, a window will open with several choices. Here, you can invite any contact you have. Should you want to invite a conferencing room, choose **Zoom Room**. You can also send an email invite to someone.

7. Once you decide who to invite, click on them and then click the **Invite** button:

Figure 1.31: Inviting meeting participants

The person or room you invited will get a meeting notification that you are inviting them to a Zoom meeting. They can accept or decline your invitation from Zoom. If an invited user is not currently logged in to Zoom, they will receive an email informing them of a missed meeting invitation:

Figure 1.32: Meeting invite

Inviting from Team Chat

1. Click the **Team Chat** icon from the top navigation screen.

2. Navigate to the person or channel whom you would like to have a meeting with. A list of people or channels is on the left navigation bar:

> **Note**
>
> To learn more about **Team Chat** channels, go to *Chapter 5, Zoom Team Chat.*

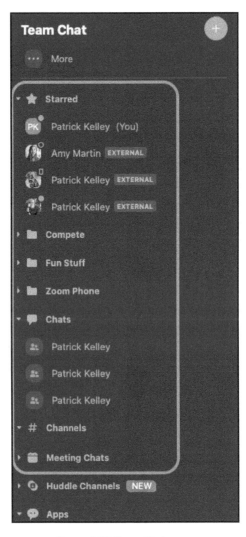

Figure 1.33: Team Chat users

3. At the top of your **Team Chat** window, you will see information about the person you are chatting with.

4. On the right side, you will see a **Camera** icon. To invite the person to a Zoom meeting, simply click it. An invitation for a Zoom audio and video meeting will be sent to the user:

Figure 1.34: Zoom meeting invite

5. Should you just want to have an audio-only meeting (no video) with a contact or user, click the up caret (^) to the right of the camera and deselect **Meet with video**. A Zoom meeting invite will be sent to the invitee.

> **Note**
> Once the invitee has accepted the Zoom audio-only meeting, they will always be given the choice to turn the camera on during the meeting later if they want.

Inviting a contact to a Zoom meeting

1. Click the **Contacts** icon from your top navigation bar.

2. Navigate to the contact you wish to meet with.

3. Click the **Meet** button to send an *audio-only* meeting invite to the user:

Figure 1.35: Contact invite

> **Note**
> Zoom by default sends an audio-only meeting when inviting someone from **Contacts**. Should anyone wish to escalate the audio meeting to a video meeting, they can choose to turn on their camera at any time.

4. An invitation to your 1:1 Zoom meeting will be sent to the invitee.

5. You now know how to invite a 1:1 contact to a Zoom meeting!

Scheduling a Zoom meeting

Now that you understand how to set up ad hoc 1:1 meetings, let's dive into how to set up scheduled meetings with individuals as well as multiple participants. Scheduled meetings are meetings that occur in the future at a pre-set time as opposed to inviting participants in real time. There are multiple ways to schedule future meetings with the Zoom client. Let's dive deeper into a few of the common ways to do that.

Scheduling Zoom meetings from the Home page

1. Click on the **Home** icon from the top navigation bar.

2. Click on the **Schedule** icon.

3. A **Schedule Meeting** window will appear, as shown here:

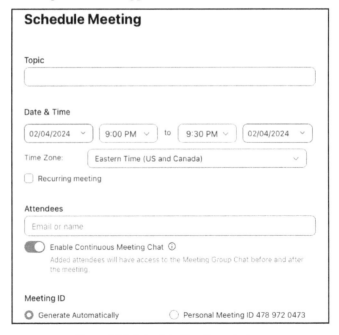

Figure 1.36: Schedule Meeting window

4. Enter the topic of your meeting (for example, **Weekly Status Meeting**).

5. Choose a date and time for the future meeting.

6. Check **Recurring meeting** if this is a meeting that will reoccur at daily, weekly, or monthly intervals.

7. Enter all the names/emails you want to be invited to the meeting in the **Attendees** area. Everyone invited will receive an email invitation to the meeting. They will be able to accept, decline, or propose a new time in the calendar invitation.

8. By default, **Enable Continuous Meeting Chat** is enabled. This creates a chat channel that allows all participants to chat before, during, and after the meeting. This is a powerful way to collaborate with invitees to the meeting. Toggle off if you don't want this feature in your meeting invite.

9. By default, an automatically generated **Meeting ID** value is chosen. You can also pick a static **Personal Meeting ID** value. For security purposes, it is best to leave this at **Generate Automatically** so that non-invited participants can't join your meeting by entering past meeting IDs you've generated.

If your organization has enabled **Templates** for meetings, you can choose one in this section. By default, this is **None**. If you are part of an organization where the Zoom admin or IT department has created templates to use, choose which one is appropriate for your meeting invite.

Note

If you have questions about which template is appropriate for your meeting, reach out to your Zoom admin for questions. Otherwise, choose **None**.

---

1. In the **Security** section, enable **Passcode**, **Waiting Room**, or both. This enhances the security of your meetings. Only invitees with the passcode can join the meeting. Invitees who don't join with the appropriate passcode are admitted to the waiting room. The meeting organizer will have the ability to admit users at their discretion.

2. By default, **Enhanced encryption** is chosen. Should you need **end-to-end encryption** (E2EE), click that option.

Note

E2EE is an advanced security feature of Zoom, encrypted with 256-bit AES GCM encryption for audio, video, and application sharing.

---

3. By default, **Video** is enabled for both the host and participants of the meeting. Toggle to off per your preference.

4. **Audio** by default is set to **Computer Audio**.

5. **Calendar** is defaulted to whichever email/calendar solution you have enabled for **Zoom Mail** and **Calendar**. You can choose between **Apple**, **Microsoft**, **Google**, or **Other**.

Interpretation is an advanced feature that allows you to assign interpreters during a meeting from one host's language to another. This feature also allows you to assign sign language interpretation. Enter the appropriate email address of the interpreters (up to 20) should you want this feature enabled.

Scheduling a Zoom meeting from the Zoom sidebar calendar

1. Navigate to the right of the Zoom client to the sidebar Zoom calendar, as shown next, and click on the icon pictured:

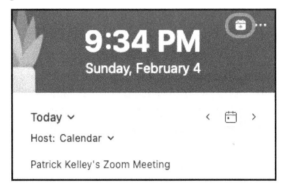

Figure 1.37: Calendar invite

2. Click the + icon. A new meeting schedule window will open:

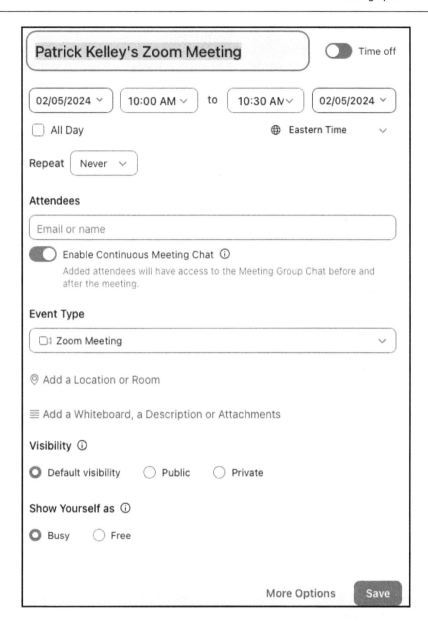

Figure 1.38: Scheduling window

3. Enter the subject of the meeting.

> **Note**
>
> If you are creating a calendar event for vacation or time off, toggle the **Time off** indicator. This will book your calendar and presence as **Off**. External people won't be able to book time with you during this period.

4. Choose the day, time, and time zone of your meeting.

5. If this will be a reoccurring meeting, choose **Repeat**, then pick how often you want the same meeting repeated (that is, **Daily**, **Weekly**, **Monthly**).

6. Enter the name or email address of all the attendees of the meeting. These can be internal or external participants.

7. By default, **Enable Continuous Meeting Chat** is toggled on. This creates a **Team Chat** channel with the same name as the meeting subject. This allows all participants in the meeting to begin sending chats before, during, or after the meeting. Chat participants can also upload files, attachments, and even agendas into the chat so that everyone is prepared for the meeting beforehand. If you don't want this feature, toggle it off.

8. Pick what type of event you want to schedule. By default, **Zoom Meeting** is chosen; however, should you have a Zoom Phone license, **Zoom Phone Call** is also a choice. If you want to book your calendar for offline purposes (that is, vacation, lunch, appointment out of the office), choose **Offline**:

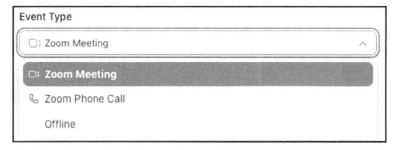

Figure 1.39: Event Type

9. By default, Zoom assumes meetings are virtual. You can add a location or room to your meeting if the Zoom meeting is being held at a physical location such as a conferencing room or office.

10. You can add whiteboards, meeting descriptions, agendas, and even attachments (that is, documents, spreadsheets, drawings) to your meeting. Click **Add Whiteboard**, **Add a description…**, or **Attachments** if you want to include these in the meeting invite. Once clicked, a new window will appear. Here, you can upload a previously created whiteboard or create a new one. You can also type in the description of what the meeting is about or an agenda. If you have any attachments for the meeting participants, these can also be uploaded:

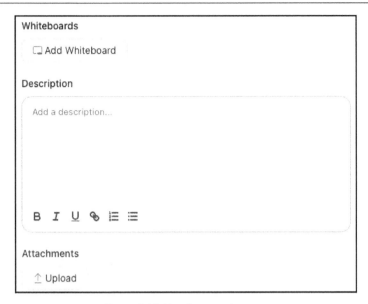

Figure 1.40: Meeting attachments

11. By default, the **Visibility** option of your meeting invite is set to **Public**. This means people with access to your calendar would be able to see all information about your meeting, such as subject, time, date, description, and attendees. Should you wish to not disclose this information, you can choose **Private**. If you choose **Private**, users will only see the meeting on your calendar as blocked off with a **Busy** message.

Note

Typically, you will want to use the **Public** visibility choice. Situations in which you would want to use **Private** would be for extra security of a meeting; for example, if you were having a meeting about yearly bonuses and didn't want anyone to know, or perhaps a private meeting with a doctor disclosing health information you want to be kept private.

---

12. By default, when you book a meeting, your calendar will show as **Busy**. Other Zoom users will see you as busy and in a meeting with a red presence indicator above your camera in Zoom or when viewing your calendar. There may be situations when you book a Zoom meeting but want to indicate you are free to contact via chat, audio, or video. Choose **Free** if you wish to appear available, even during a Zoom meeting.

13. Should you need additional meeting configuration, click **More Options**. This will open an expanded window with all of the meeting options available from the preceding recipe, *Setting up a Zoom Meeting*.

Creating a Zoom meeting from the calendar

1. Click the **Calendar** icon at the top navigation bar.

2. At the top of the screen, click the blue **+ New Event** button:

Figure 1.41: + New Event button

3. After clicking the **+ New Event** button, a new Zoom meeting schedule window will appear.

4. All the configuration options that were discussed appear here in order to set up your new Zoom meeting.

> Note
>
> No matter which of the aforementioned methods you choose to create a Zoom meeting, the post-invite actions are the same:
>
> - An email will be sent to all meeting invitees. Meeting invitees will have the opportunity to accept or decline the meeting.
>
> - If the meeting is accepted, the meeting will appear in the attendee's calendar.
>
> - If the meeting is declined, the meeting will be removed from the attendee's calendar.
>
> - The organizer of the meeting will receive updates from all attendees when they accept or decline the meeting.

2

Content Sharing and Collaboration

Content sharing is a vital part of Zoom. Content can be defined as presentation material such as a PowerPoint slide or a Google Doc. You can also share your desktop or screen, even a Zoom whiteboard. Zoom allows users to share videos or audio such as music. You can share applications or portions of your screen. You can also share content from your iPhone or iPad. If you want to get even more advanced, Zoom allows you to use PowerPoint slides as a virtual background with your video in front. Sometimes it may be necessary to use a second camera when presenting with a physical whiteboard or a real prototype on a desk. The point is, when you are trying to convey a critical message to your meeting attendees, sharing content is vital.

In this chapter, you will learn all the ways Zoom allows you to share content during a meeting, which will allow your meeting participants to see exactly what you are saying and describing, immersing your attendees using more than just your words. Bringing your audience visually into the meeting allows you to dive deeper into the narrative of your message. These could be the most vital recipes of the cookbook.

In this chapter, we're going to cover the following recipes:

- Sharing content in a Zoom meeting
- Changing layouts
- Creating whiteboards
- Sharing whiteboards
- Presenting whiteboards
- Sharing content via the iPhone/iPad
- Sharing audio during a Zoom meeting
- Sharing video

- Using slides as a Virtual Background

- Sharing a portion of your screen

- Sharing a single application in a meeting

- Pausing screen sharing

Technical requirements

As a best practice, always update your Zoom to the latest version before beginning:

1. Click on the profile icon in the top-right corner and choose **Check for Updates**:

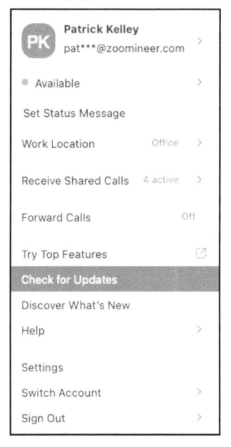

Figure 2.1: Check for Updates

2. Your Zoom client will check to see if there is a new update. If there is, click the **Update** button.

Sharing content in a Zoom meeting

Sharing content during a meeting is the cornerstone of presenting beyond just your audio and video. Presenting to meeting attendees while adding some visual context to the point you are trying to convey could be one of the most important features of Zoom. In this recipe, you will learn how to share content in a meeting.

How to do it...

1. Start or join a Zoom meeting.
2. Once you have joined the meeting, you will see a **Share Screen** icon in the bottom navigation bar. This icon is highlighted in green for easy visual reference.

Figure 2.2: Share Screen icon

3. Notice the up caret (^) to the right of the **Share Screen** icon. As a meeting organizer, you have control over who can share during a meeting, with the option to choose between one person at a time or multiple. As a meeting attendee, you will **not** have this option.

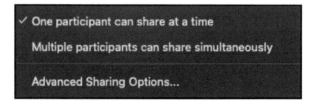

Figure 2.3: Sharing rights for participants

4. When you are ready to share content during a meeting, click the **Share Screen** icon. A menu of choices will appear.

> **Note**
> We will dive deeper into each of the features beyond just the desktop in future recipes. For now, we will focus on sharing a desktop.

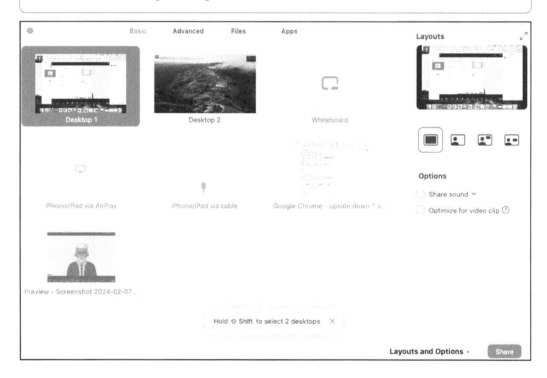

Figure 2.4: Share Screen

5. Zoom allows you to share up to two desktops at a time. By default, Desktop 1 is chosen to share. If you note in *Figure 2.4*, you will see **Desktop 1** highlighted in blue. If you have multiple monitors, you will see each desktop as an individual choice to share. Sometimes it is helpful to share content from one desktop while viewing the Zoom meeting from another desktop. Sharing a desktop is the most common item shared during Zoom meetings.

> **Note**
>
> If you wish to share two desktops, you can press the *Shift* key and pick which desktops you would like to share.

6. Click the **Share** button on the bottom-right corner after choosing which desktop(s) to share.

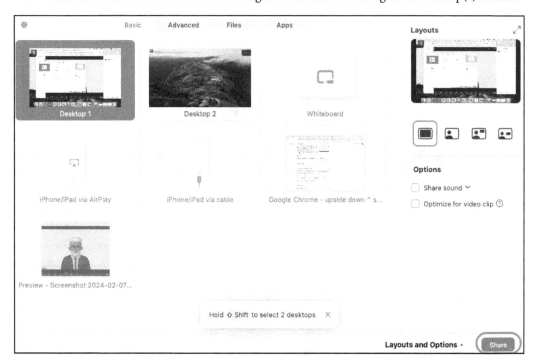

Figure 2.5: The Share button

7.   You will be given two notifications of what you are sharing during a meeting. First, the desktop you are sharing will be highlighted with a green border around what is being shared.

Figure 2.6: Green screen border

The second notification is a preview screen indicating what attendees of the meeting are viewing. This is a dropdown from your **Meetings Control** bar, as shown in the following screenshot.

Figure 2.7: Screen Share Preview

Changing layouts

By default, Zoom shares the full screen of any desktop you share. You may wish to change this with the *layout* feature. This feature lets you share your content in multiple ways, enhancing your presentation.

How to do it...

1. Click the **Share Screen** icon during a meeting.
2. Once the **Share Screen** options window appears, you will see **Layouts** to the right of the window as pictured in the following screenshot.

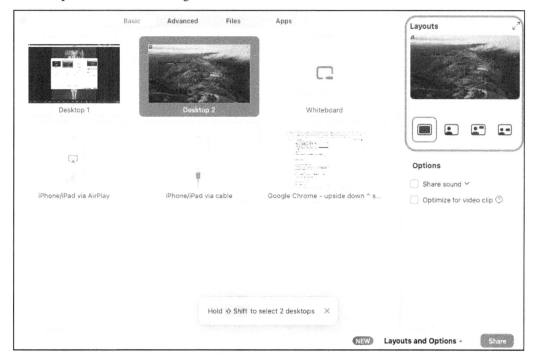

Figure 2.8: Layouts

3. There are four options to choose from:

- **Full screen**: This displays your entire desktop.

Figure 2.9: Full screen

- **Video hover**: This mode displays your entire desktop with your video overlayed on top.

Note

If you click and hold the left mouse button on your video, you can move it anywhere on the screen from the **Layouts** window!

Figure 2.10: Video hover mode

- **Video and full screen**: In this mode, your video and your full screen share are separated.

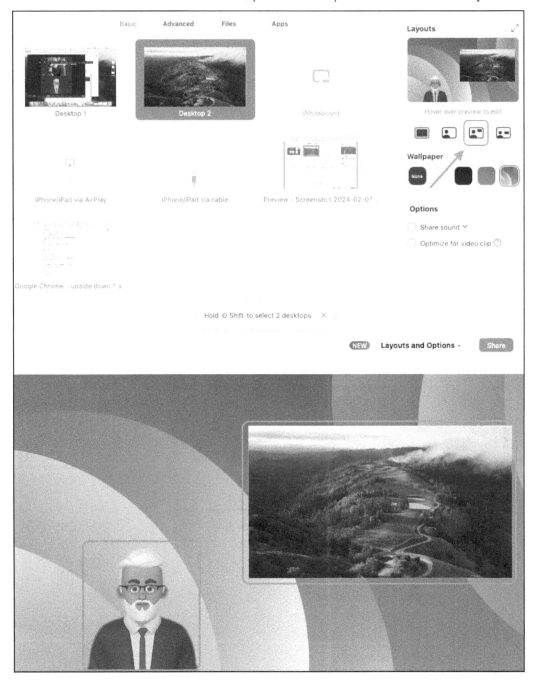

Figure 2.11: Sharing a video and the full screen

Note

In this mode, you can also change the wallpaper behind your video and screen share with the **Wallpaper** option, as pictured in the following figure. You have the option to choose one of five wallpaper choices.

Figure 2.12: Wallpaper

- **Side by side**: In this mode, both your video and screenshare are laid out in the middle of your screen.

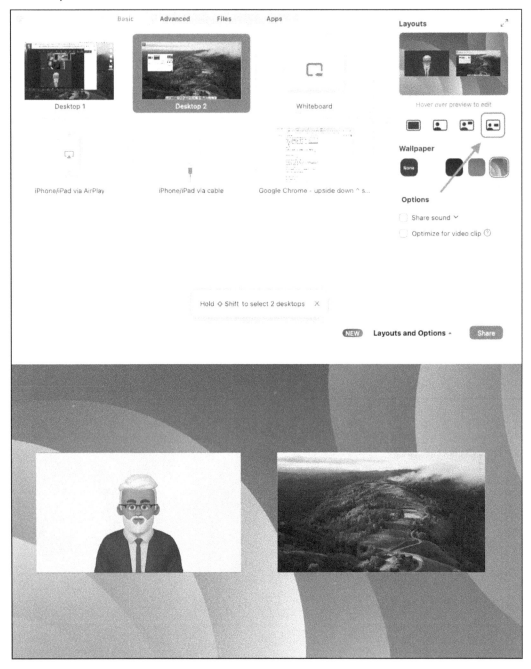

Figure 2.13: Side by side

There's more...

You can adjust the size and position of both your video and screen share from the **Layouts** preview screen in any mode.

Figure 2.14: Layouts preview screen

Creating Zoom whiteboards

Sharing content from a desktop or application is certainly an effective means of presenting data. However, sometimes we need to be creative or spontaneous as we work, such as when trying to come up with ideas with a team, or simply drawing something out to direct energy for free-flowing thoughts.

Zoom includes whiteboarding features to brainstorm and collaborate on a digital canvas. Zoom Whiteboard is a powerful tool that allows users to engage others with an expandable and persistent digital experience that is intuitive with advanced features. The whiteboard allows both in-person and remote teams the ability to ideate visually with ideas, drawings, shapes, and more.

Zoom created whiteboards with a unified space so individuals and teams could visually structure their thoughts on a persistent online digital surface. Whiteboard enables dynamic collaboration with enhanced flexibility. Whiteboards can be easily shared before, during, and after a meeting.

Getting ready

Navigate to the **Whiteboards** icon from Zoom's top navigation bar and click on it.

Figure 2.15: Zoom Whiteboards

There are three ways to create a whiteboard. You can either create a new whiteboard with a blank canvas, use a precreated template, or open a previously created whiteboard. Let's cover these methods.

How to do it...

1. To create a new blank whiteboard, click the **New** button at the top-right corner of your screen.

Figure 2.16: The New button

2. A **Templates** window will appear. This will allow you to pick from precreated whiteboard templates such as brainstorming, design, even strategy, and planning. These choices will appear on the left of the screen. Click any template that fits the whiteboard design you require.

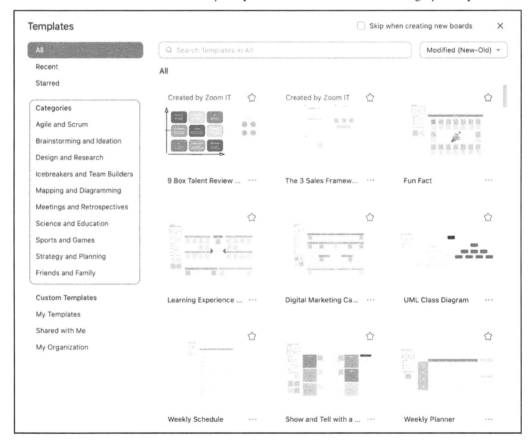

Figure 2.17: Whiteboard templates

> **Note**
>
> Templates are designed to take a lot of the effort out of creating new designs from scratch. They are pre-built to help you customize them to your needs. All templates can be modified after they are created, so be sure to experiment with them to kick-start your whiteboards.

3. If you would like to create your own blank whiteboard from scratch, just close the **Templates** window and navigate to the drawing tools on the left of your screen.

4. The drawing toolbar appears once your whiteboard appears. This toolbar contains all the tools you need to create a whiteboard.

Figure 2.18: Drawing tools

Sharing whiteboards

You can create Zoom whiteboards on your own, but you can also collaborate with an entire team of contributors during a brainstorming session, for instance, with your meeting attendees. Whiteboards are a creative way to collaborate, and you will want to most likely share your whiteboard with other co-workers or external contacts after you are done.

How to do it...

1. Open any whiteboard that you created from scratch or from a template from the **Whiteboard** icon in the top navigation bar in your Zoom client.

2. Click the **Share** button at the top-right corner of your whiteboard.

Figure 2.19: Whiteboard Share button

3. A **Share Whiteboard** window will appear giving you the ability to send this whiteboard to other participants for review, comment, or editing.

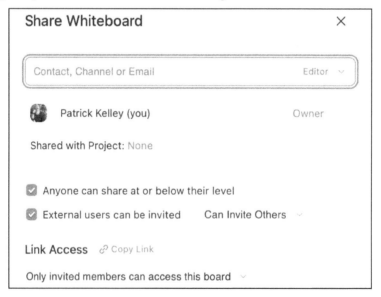

Figure 2.20: Share Whiteboard permissions screen

4. You can now enter all the contacts, emails, or even Team Chat channels you wish to share the whiteboard with.

5. After you have entered all the names with whom you want to share your whiteboard, you can control the permissions for your whiteboard with the drop-down menu from the right of the names. There are four choices:

- **Co-Owner**: Users with link access can have the same permissions as the original board owner, including sharing, editing, commenting, and deleting

- **Editor**: Users with link access can edit the board

- **Commenter**: Users with link access can comment on the board

- **Viewer**: Users with link access can view the board

6. Once you have chosen the appropriate permissions for your whiteboard, you can now enter an invite message. This is optional, but is helpful to people receiving the whiteboard so they can quickly scan what the whiteboard is about.

Figure 2.21: Whiteboard permissions and invite message

7. By default, anyone can share the whiteboard with other people at or below their level. For example, if you added a user with **Commenter** rights, they would only be able to share the same whiteboard with others at the **Commenter** or **Viewer** levels. If you wish that no one be able to share the whiteboard then this option can be unchecked.

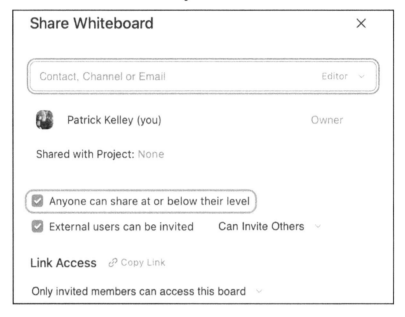

Figure 2.22: Whiteboard permissions

8. By default, external users can be invited to a whiteboard and these users have the option to invite other users or not, depending on their permissions. This is helpful when collaborating with other companies or teams outside your organization. If you wish to keep this whiteboard available only inside your organization, the following option can be left unchecked.

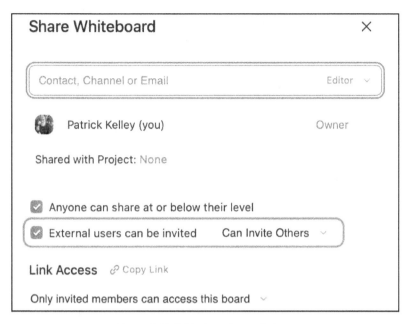

Figure 2.23: Whiteboard permissions

9. By default, only people who have been invited to the whiteboard will have access. However, this can be changed. There are three options. Choose the appropriate permission level for your whiteboard:

- Only invited members have access

- Anyone in your organization

- Anyone with the link to the whiteboard can view it

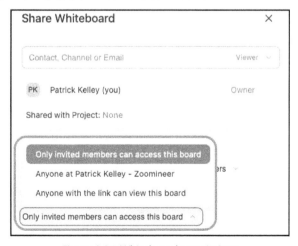

Figure 2.24: Whiteboard permissions

10. Once all your permissions have been set and all the people and/or channels you want invited to the meeting have been entered, you can click the **Share Whiteboard** button. Users will be notified via both email and a chat message in Zoom.

Figure 2.25: Share Whiteboard

11. That's it! You now know how to share whiteboards in Zoom.

Presenting whiteboards

In the previous recipe, you learned how to present content such as your desktop during a Zoom meeting. This applies to whiteboards as well. You have multiple options to present a whiteboard to your attendees. You can present the content of a new whiteboard or a previously created one. You can also present a new or existing whiteboard in collaboration mode, allowing all meeting attendees to brainstorm and create content on the whiteboard simultaneously.

Method 1 – from the Basic tab

How to do it...

1. Start a new Zoom meeting or join an existing one.

2. Navigate to the **Share Screen** icon.

3. You will be presented with the **Basic** tab screen with items to share. Choose **Whiteboard**.

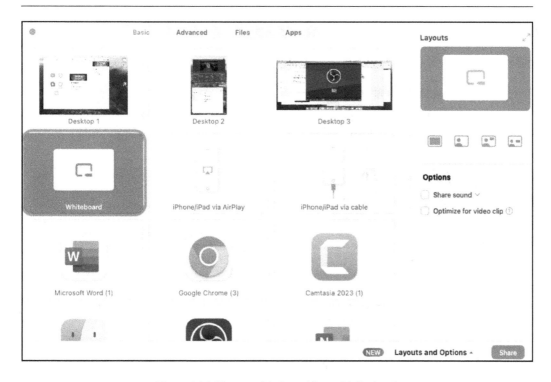

Figure 2.26: Share a whiteboard from the Basic tab

4. A new whiteboard will be created and shared with everyone in the meeting. By default, the organizer of the meeting is the owner of the whiteboard. Also by default, all meeting attendees the editors of the whiteboard. This allows everyone to collaborate and brainstorm together on the same whiteboard simultaneously.

5. This whiteboard can also be shared as you learned in the previous recipe. This is helpful should you want further collaboration on the whiteboard to take place and be saved after the meeting. If you were using the whiteboard to just quickly clarify a point or something that was ephemeral, you can stop your share or close your whiteboard and it will disappear.

6. Should you wish to share your whiteboard during the meeting, navigate to the upper-right corner of your whiteboard and choose **Share**, as you learned in the previous recipe.

Figure 2.27: Share Whiteboard

Method 2 – using the Whiteboards app

How to do it...

1. Start a new Zoom meeting or join an existing one.

2. Navigate to the **Whiteboards** app on the **Meetings Control** bar at the bottom of your meeting window. Click on **Whiteboards** and you will be given a choice to create a **New Whiteboard** or share an **Existing Whiteboard** that was previously created.

Figure 2.28: Whiteboard shared from Meeting Control

3. By choosing **New Whiteboard**, a blank whiteboard with no content is created for meeting participants to use.

4. Choosing **Existing Whiteboard** brings up a new window displaying all previously created Whiteboards. Click the one you wish to share.

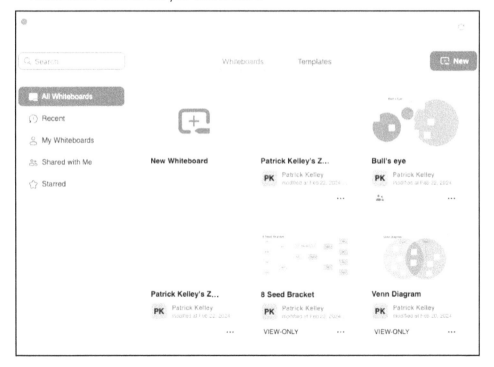

Figure 2.29: Existing whiteboard

5. Once you have chosen the whiteboard you wish to share, an additional menu will appear concerning how you wish to open the board.

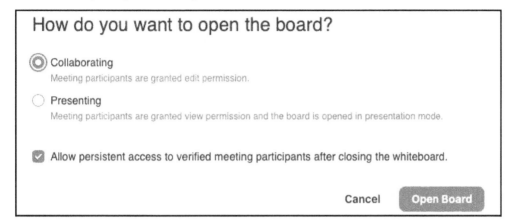

Figure 2.30: Opening the whiteboard

> **Note**
>
> **Collaborating** mode is chosen by default. This allows all meeting attendees the ability to create content and edit on the whiteboard you are sharing.
>
> **Presenting** mode grants meeting attendees the ability to view the whiteboard with no ability to create or edit.
>
> If you want your whiteboard to persist after the meeting for further brainstorming or collaboration with meeting partipants, check the **Allow persistent access to verified meeting participants after closing the whiteboard** option.

6. You also have advanced sharing options for the whiteboard. To adjust these settings, go to the ^ icon to the right of the **Whiteboards** button in your Zoom meeting window.

Figure 2.31: Advanced whiteboard sharing options button

7. Now the **Advanced sharing options** window will appear with the following options:

    - **Allow participants to share whiteboard** is toggled *on* by default. If this is toggled *off* only the host of the meeting can share whiteboards during the meeting.

    - **Who can start sharing when someone else is sharing?** By default, **Host only** is selected. If you wish all participants to be able to start sharing when someone else is sharing, choose **All participants**.

    - **Who can initiate new whiteboard in the meeting?** By default, **All participants** can begin sharing a whiteboard during a meeting.

Figure 2.32: Advanced sharing options

You're now an expert on how to share and present whiteboards!

Sharing content via the iPhone/iPad

There may be times when you wish to share content from an iPad or iPhone directly into a Zoom meeting. For example, you might have a picture on your iPhone that you would like to share in a meeting with your attendees. Another example is you may be in a conferencing room and want to share a presentation from your iPad. The examples are limitless, but all are possible with Zoom.

How to do it...

1. Start or join a Zoom meeting.

2. Navigate to the **Share Screen** icon on the bottom of your **Menu Control** bar.

Figure 2.33: Share Screen

3. A **Basic** sharing window will appear. There are two options to share from your iPhone/iPad. On the sharing screen, you have the option to either share content via AirPlay or through a cable connection.

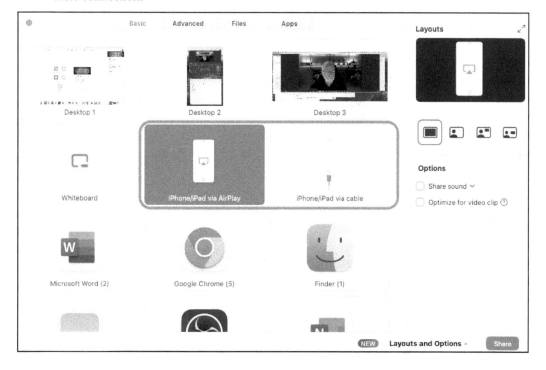

Figure 2.34: Share content from iPhone/iPad

4. The first method is **iPhone/iPad via AirPlay**. This method uses a wireless network that the computer and iPhone/iPad are connected to.

> **Note**
>
> Both the Mac/PC and iPhone/iPad *must* be on the exact same network for this method to work. This is most likely the case when you are in your home office or have both your computer and iPhone connected to the same wireless network in a work setting.

5. Click on **iPhone/iPad via AirPlay** and it will be highlighted in blue. Then click the **Share** button.

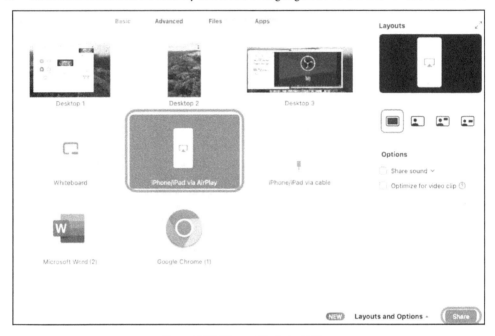

Figure 2.35: iPhone/iPad via AirPlay

6. Directions will appear on your screen on how to proceed. As noted above, make sure your Mac and your iPhone/iPad are connected to the same wireless network. (Note: Airplay is an Apple feature. This option isn't available on a PC).

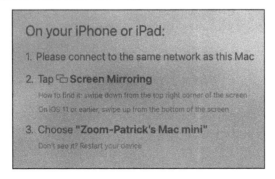

Figure 2.36: Share from iPhone/iPad via AirPlay directions

7.   On your iPhone/iPad, tap **Screen Mirroring**.

Figure 2.37: Screen Mirroring

8. Refer to *Figure 2.33* in *step 3* to find the AirPlay device you need to connect to. In the example provided, it's listed as **Zoom-Patrick's Mac mini**. Simply tap on this device name on your iPhone/iPad to establish the connection.

Figure 2.38: iPhone/iPad via AirPlay device

9. Your iPhone/iPad screen will now be shared in your Zoom meeting and all attendees will be able to see your device's screen.

> **Note**
>
> The orientation of the device matters. For example, if you're using your iPhone and rotate the device 90 degrees to share content in Portrait mode, what appears upright to you will be displayed in Landscape mode to others. The following figure illustrates this difference when sharing the Calculator screen from an iPhone in a Zoom meeting.

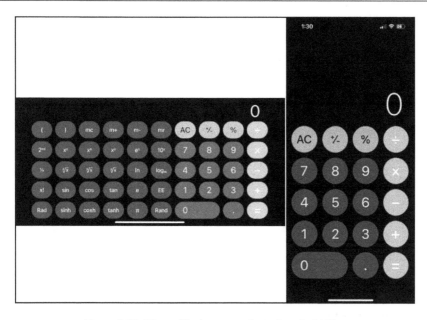

Figure 2.39: iPhone/iPad screen orientation via AirPlay

10. If you want to use a cable instead of AirPlay, choose the **iPhone/iPad via cable** option, then click **Share**. (Note: This option is only available on a Mac.)

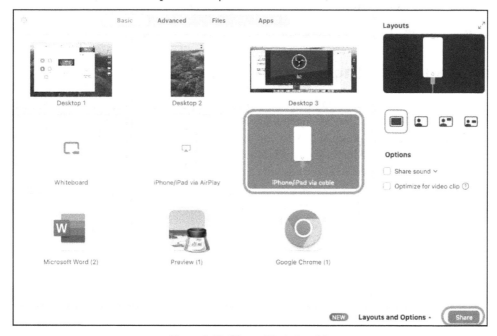

Figure 2.40: iPhone/iPad via cable

11. A instruction window will appear.

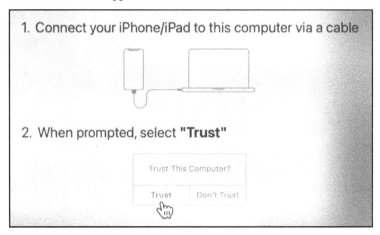

Figure 2.41: iPhone/iPad via cable instructions

12. Connect your device to your computer via the appropriate cable.

13. The first time you connect your iPhone or iPad to your computer you will be prompted, **Trust This Computer**. Tap **Trust** to continue. (**Note**: This step will only happen once – if you have previously trusted the connected computer from your device, the iPad/iPhone screen will immediately be shared to your Zoom meeting without this prompt).

That's it! You've mastered how to share your iPhone or iPad to a Zoom meeting.

Sharing audio during a Zoom meeting

At times it is helpful to share your computer audio during a meeting. For example, at the beginning of a meeting, you could play music for the first few minutes while people are joining the meeting. Sometimes it is awkward for a group of people who may not know each other to just stare at a screen with unfamiliar faces silently. Music can help! Maybe you want to play an audio clip from a podcast or speech. All can easily be done in Zoom with the audio sharing feature.

How to do it...

1. Start or join a Zoom meeting.

2. Navigate to the **Share Screen** icon on your **Meetings Control** bar.

Figure 2.42 Share Screen

3. Click the **Advanced** tab on the top of your share window. Then navigate to the **Computer Audio** option and click on it. It will be highlighted in blue as pictured in the following figure. (**Note**: Notice in the bottom-right corner of the **Computer Audio** option, there is a drop-down carot ˅. Click this to choose between **Mono** sound or **Stereo (High-fidelity)**. If you are sharing simple audio, such as sounds or speech, you can leave this on the **Mono** option. If you are playing music, you would most likely want to choose Stereo.)

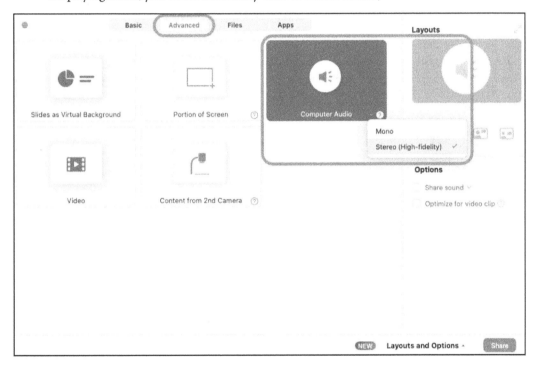

Figure 2.43: Computer Audio

4. Now any sound that you play from your computer (music, speech, effects, etc.) will be heard by your meeting attendees. You can verify you are sharing computer sound by looking at the top of your Zoom meeting window. Highlighted in green it indicates you are sharing computer sound. You can stop sharing sound at any time by clicking **Stop Share**.

Figure 2.44: Stop Share

There's more...

There is an additional way to share sound should you wish to have audio in addition to presenting your desktop or application. For example, you might have a slide deck that has music and voiceover audio and you want to share both at the same time with your attendees.

From the **Share** window, choose the **Basic** tab, and navigate to the right-hand panel where it says **Options** as shown in the following figure. You will see a **Share sound** option. Check the box, and choose what you would like to present.

In the following example, **Desktop 1** and **Share sound** are both checked. Now meeting attendees will see Desktop 1 as well as any corresponding audio once you click **Share**.

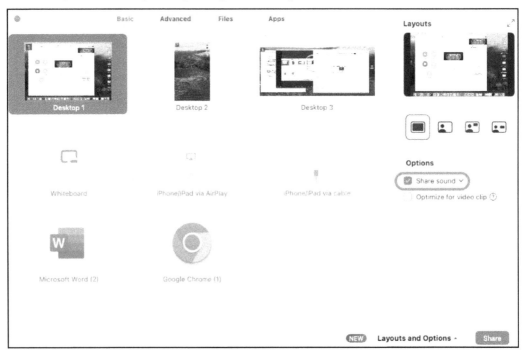

Figure 2.45: Share sound

You've now mastered how to share your computer audio during a Zoom meeting.

Sharing a video

Sometimes it is helpful to share a video during a meeting. It's great to share your desktop, whiteboard, or audio as you've learned in previous recipes, but videos are another awesome way to keep your attendees engaged and immersed in your presentation. Zoom can easily play video as well as audio for all your meeting participants.

How to do it...

1. Start or join a Zoom meeting.
2. Navigate to the **Share Screen** icon on your **Meetings Control** bar.
3. Navigate to the **Advanced** tab and choose **Video**. It will be highlighted in blue once clicked.

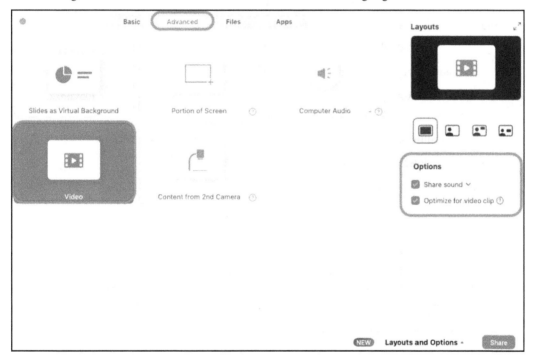

Figure 2.46: Share Video

> **Note**
>
> Notice in **Options** that the **Share Sound** and **Optimize for video clip** are on by default.
>
> If you don't want sound in your video, you can uncheck the **Share sound** option.
>
> It is generally recommended to use the **Optimize for video clip** option for sharing videos. This restricts and downscales the resolution to 1080/720 to provide improved quality. This can be unchecked to allow for higher resolution, but this should only be used in situations where framerate is less important. So basically, just leave it checked!

4. Now click **Share**.

5. Navigate to the video you wish to share from your computer from the browser window that opened.

6. You can also share videos from streaming providers such as YouTube or Netflix.

7. Your video will appear with playback controls. These controls are not visible to other meeting participants while you play your video. You will have the following controls:

    -   **Play/Pause**: Start or pause the playback of the video

    -   **Elapsed time/total video length**: Shows the current elapsed time of video playback, and the total length of the video file

    -   **Playback slider**: Allows you to skip to other points of the video playback range

    -   **Volume**: Allows you to adjust the volume of the video being shared

    -   **Fullscreen**: Allows you to make the video full-screen for you and viewers

There's more...

Remember how to change the layouts of your Zoom meeting as you learned in the previous recipe? This still applies here too. You can play your video in full screen of course, but you can also have your video play side by side with your own camera feed, for example. All are still options when sharing a video. Look at the following examples of layouts. Have fun with it. Make your presentations even better with the knowledge you've learned!

Figure 2.47: Video sharing layouts

Now you have mastered how to share a video in Zoom! Your Jedi powers are strong!

Using slides as a Virtual Background

Presenting content is a very powerful tool when using Zoom. One of the best tools to use when presenting is Microsoft PowerPoint. You can use PowerPoint to create stunning visual slide decks, with slides that have text, graphics, and even video and audio all in one application. Zoom allows you to harness the ability of PowerPoint to present both your slides and your camera video feed at the same time! Using a super cool Zoom sharing feature, you can now use your own PowerPoint slides as a visual backdrop while you present. Learn how next!

How to do it...

1. Start or join a Zoom meeting.

2. Navigate to the **Share Screen** icon on your **Meetings Control** bar.

3. Go to the **Advanced** tab and click **Slides as Virtual Background**. Once it is highlighted in blue, click **Share**.

4. A file browser window will open. Navigate to the PowerPoint deck you want to use as a Virtual Background. Click **Open**.

5. You will now be sharing the PowerPoint deck with your video superimposed over the top.

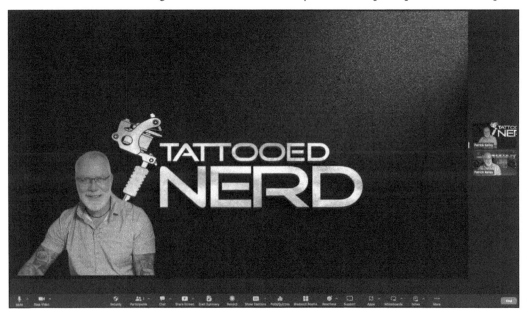

Figure 2.48: Virtual Background slide

Using your slides as a virtual background? Super cool!

There's more...

1. As the presenter, look at the bottom middle of your Zoom meeting screen. You will see the slide controls for your PowerPoint deck. In the following example, there are three slides in the deck, and I can navigate through them using the < and > buttons to move forward or back.

Figure 2.49: Virtual Background slide controls

2. Notice the **...** button to the right of your slide numbers. This provides additional controls for your video. Click on it to view more options.

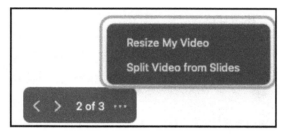

Figure 2.50: Extended video controls

3. Choose the **Resize My Video** option. Your camera video will now be outlined in blue lines. Drag the corners to make your video bigger or smaller for your presentation.

4. Click and hold your camera video to reposition it anywhere on the screen. Zoom makes presenting a breeze!

5. If you would like to stop using your camera feed during your PowerPoint presentation, just choose **Split Video from Slides**. This will stop your camera video and only share your slides.

6. Should you want to begin showing your camera video again, click **...** and then choose **Merge Video and Slides**.

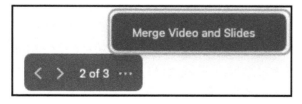

Figure 2.51: Video controls

You've now learned how to use PowerPoint slides as a Virtual Background during Zoom meeting presentations. You are becoming amazing at this!

Sharing a portion of your screen

There may be times when you would like to share just a part of your screen or desktop. For example, I use a large 50" monitor as my main screen and run multiple applications at the same time. Sharing my entire desktop would be too much information for a meeting attendee. I might just want to share a small part of my screen, such as an application, picture, or code. Zoom has this feature and it's very helpful when presenting.

How to do it...

1. Start or join a Zoom meeting.

2. Navigate to the **Share Screen** icon on your **Meetings Control** bar.

3. Click on the **Advanced** tab of your share screen window. Then click **Portion of Screen**. It will be highlighted in blue. Then click **Share**.

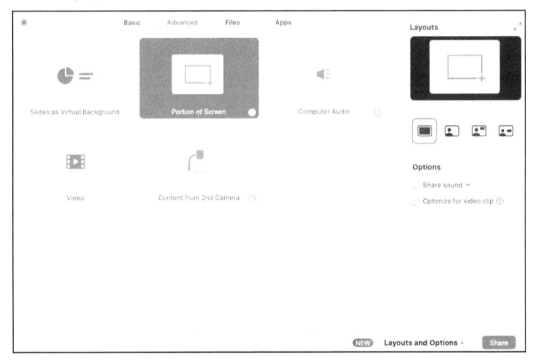

Figure 2.52: Share a portion of the screen

4. A green border outline will now appear on your screen. Anything within this border is shared with your meeting attendees.

Figure 2.53: Sharing a portion of the screen

There's more...

You can adjust this border to any size. Just click on the edges or corners and drag and drop to any size that works for you.

You can also click and hold the mouse button on the thicker top green border to move the border around your screen. It's amazing and super flexible for anything you may want to share.

You are becoming a Zoom master at sharing. Congratulations!

Sharing a single application in a meeting

There may be times when you only want to share a single application rather than your entire desktop. For example, I run several applications simultaneously, such as Microsoft Word, Google Slides, and a web browser. If I were to share my desktop my meeting attendees would see all these applications at the same time, probably not very helpful if I just want to present a Google Slides deck for a presentation. Zoom can share a single application from any desktop. It's pretty cool.

How to do it...

1. Start or join a Zoom meeting.
2. Navigate to the **Share Screen** icon on your **Meetings Control** bar.
3. From the **Basic** share screen window, you see all the applications that you have open on your computer. In the following example, I am running Microsoft Word, Acrobat Reader, and Microsoft PowerPoint. I have chosen to share just my Microsoft PowerPoint application by clicking on it. Notice it's highlighted in blue and appears in the **Layouts** screen. Choose which application you wish to share, and then click **Share**.

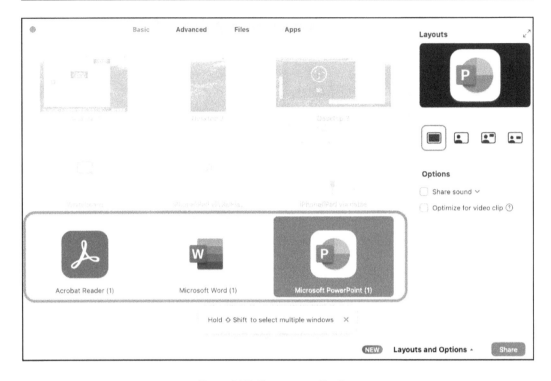

Figure 2.54: Share an application

4. Now only the application you selected to share will be viewable by your meeting attendees. Notice the application you selected is highlighted in green, indicating what you're sharing and what your attendees are seeing.

5. Should you wish to change the application you are sharing, you can easily start a new share.

6. Navigate to your Meetings Control bar. Click the **New Share** icon.

Figure 2.55: New Share

7. The **Basic** screen share window will reopen. Choose the new application you wish to share, and then click **Share**.

8. Well done…you now know how to share an app!

> **Note**
> Don't forget about layouts! You still have the ability to change the look of your Zoom meeting presentations with this tool, changing your camera video position as well as your application during your share.

Pausing screen sharing

Sometimes during a meeting, you may be sharing your desktop and dragging in multiple applications to share. You might not wish to have your attendees watch as you move windows around your screen during your screen-sharing presentation. This can be resolved with the **Pause Share** feature. This allows you to stop sharing momentarily and then resume your screen share when you're ready.

How to do it...

1. After you start sharing a screen, the **Pause Share** icon appears. **Click** it to pause your screen share.

Figure 2.56: Pause Share

2. This will stop your screen share for all meeting participants.
3. To resume sharing your screen, click the **Resume Share** icon.

Figure 2.57: Resume Share

4. With that, you've mastered pausing your share!

3
Managing Zoom Meetings

Zoom offers much more than simple audio and video meetings. It is an immersive and incredibly effective collaboration and communication platform. Properly using all the meeting tools will make you extremely efficient at hosting and presenting fantastic meetings. Allowing your attendees to stay engaged and continually learn from you during your meetings is the goal of this chapter.

We will dive deeper into the power of Zoom beyond audio, video, and content sharing. As a presenter and meeting organizer, you have an obligation to your audience to keep them informed before, during, and after the meeting with things such as agendas, notes, and meeting content. You want to fully utilize your audience's attention and time. We are going to introduce how to take persistent notes through the entire meeting life cycle, as well as how to use reactions to prompt feedback or provide silent encouragement and applause. Sometimes, the most effective way to communicate is via Chat during a meeting. At other times, you may wish to even annotate on a screenshare with drawing tools and symbols. Using proper agendas is vital when sending out meeting invites to fully convey why you are even scheduling a meeting. And no one likes a meeting that runs longer than planned. Keep everyone on track with meeting timers. How many times have you heard an attendee's dog bark or a hungry child ask for more cereal during an important presentation because Mute wasn't on? Finally, you will learn how to properly use virtual backgrounds during your meeting, either for branding or because you maybe forgot to make the bed and you don't want anyone to see.

In this chapter, we're going to cover the following main recipes:

- Using Zoom Notes
- Using reactions
- Using meeting chat
- Using annotations
- Using meeting timers
- Using the mute feature
- Implementing virtual backgrounds

Technical requirements

As a best practice, always update your Zoom to the latest version. I've explained how to check Zoom updates in the *Technical requirements* section of *Chapter 2*.

Using Zoom Notes

Zoom Notes allows users to collaborate during the entire meeting life cycle (before, during, and after a meeting). This helps drive the productivity of all meeting attendees. Notes is a workspace to create and share content, either from within a Zoom meeting or asynchronously before or after a meeting. This helps eliminate the distraction of having to switch applications to take notes during a meeting – no more going to Microsoft Word or Google Docs while you are on a Zoom call. You can take notes right inside the Zoom client using Zoom Notes. You can even share notes with all meeting participants for further collaboration and real-time feedback. Notes offers a seamless way to create agendas, take notes, and create content, all while staying within the Zoom platform:

- *Before a meeting*: Create notes, build agendas, and share them with meeting invitees in advance of the meeting to relay ideas and information

- *During a meeting*: Create a new note while in a Zoom meeting and share it with attendees to collaborate and keep everyone informed

- *After a meeting*: Share information with all the meeting participants, or even users who weren't in the meeting but could benefit from the information

Zoom Notes in a meeting

How to do it...

1. Start or join a Zoom meeting.

2. Navigate to the **Notes** icon on the **Meeting Control** bar:

Figure 3.1: Zoom Notes

3. Notice the ^ to the right of the **Notes** icon. This allows you to control who can share notes during a meeting:

Figure 3.2: Zoom Notes

4. Once you click the **Notes** icon, a **Notes** window will open to the right of your Zoom meeting:

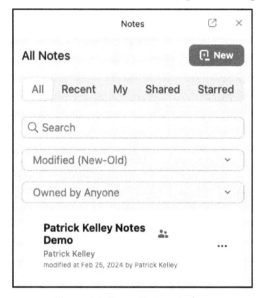

Figure 3.3: Zoom Notes window

5. All Zoom notes previously created by or shared with you are accessible. Notice the **Recent**, **My**, **Shared**, and **Starred** tabs. You can easily navigate to these sections and share notes with all meeting participants. If this is the first time you have used Notes, click the blue **New** button to create a new note for your meeting:

Figure 3.4: New Zoom note

6. A rich text editor window will appear. This allows you to format your notes any way you want by switching fonts, colors, numbers, bullet lists, and more. By default, the meeting you created will be named using either your personal meeting name (if it was an ad-hoc-created meeting) or the name you scheduled the meeting with. Feel free to click on any part of the name if you want to rename your Zoom note appropriately:

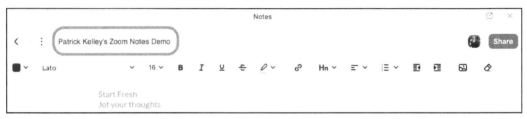

Figure 3.5: Zoom Notes editor

> **Note**
> You can resize the Notes window by clicking on the left border of the note and dragging it left or right to make it bigger or smaller.

7. At any time during the meeting, you can share your notes. It is helpful to share your notes at the beginning of the meeting to keep all participants abreast of the information as well as allow attendees to contribute to note-taking. Click the **Share** button to instantly share a note:

Figure 3.6: Share button

8. A **Share Note** window will appear. Enter any names, channels, or emails you wish to share the Zoom note with. Notice that to the right of where you entered the names, you can change permissions on the notes as well. You would most likely want to share the Zoom note with all meeting participants during a meeting. You can easily do that by clicking on the **Share to Meeting** link. By default, **Anyone can share at or below their level** is checked. This can be changed by unchecking this choice. Also, **External users can be invited** is on by default. As the Note creator, you can adjust this as well to limit note visibility:

Figure 3.7: Share Zoom notes

9.   At the bottom of the **Share Notes** window, you also have **Link Access**. This gives you the ability to share notes via the Notes link as well as control access:

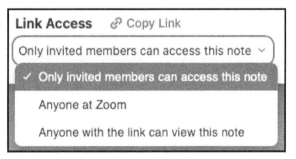

Figure 3.8: Link Access

Zoom Notes outside a Zoom meeting

How to do it...

10. Navigate to the **Notes** icon from the top navigation bar of your Zoom client and click on it:

Figure 3.9: Zoom Notes application

> **Note**
>
> Did you know you can rearrange the top navigation bar icons? Simply click and hold down your left mouse button on any icon and drag it left or right to reposition it! This is super helpful to keep your most used Zoom apps at the top of your navigation bar.

11. A **Zoom Notes** window will open. This contains all the notes you've created previously as well as all notes that have been shared with you:

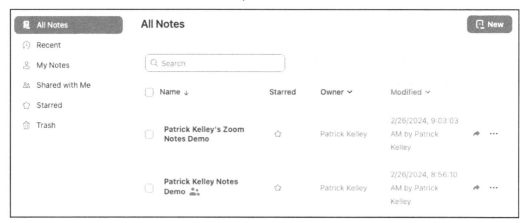

Figure 3.10: Zoom Notes application

12. You can navigate to any note you wish from the left navigation tabs. Click any note to open, edit, or share accordingly.

13. You can also create new Zoom notes from this screen by clicking the blue **New** button:

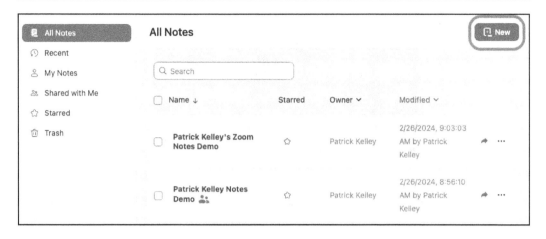

Figure 3.11: New button

You've now become a Zoom Notes master!

> **Note**
>
> Zoom Notes is a powerful tool to use before, during, or after meetings. A great tip would be to create your meeting agenda in Zoom Notes, then copy and send the Zoom Notes link in your meeting invite. That way, everyone invited is informed of what the meeting is concerning and can even contribute to the agenda by collaborating on the notes. This creates a very immersive effect for your meeting, allowing everyone to contribute to its success.

Using reactions in a Zoom meeting

It is helpful to interact with meeting attendees in a non-verbal fashion. For example, the presenter might have shared content during the meeting that everyone loves, and the attendees want to react in an enthusiastic way with non-verbal feedback such as applause or celebration emojis. Perhaps the speaker is talking too fast to understand and you would like to request them to slow down. You can even raise your hand to ask a question. All of these options are possible with the *Zoom reactions* tool.

How to do it...

1. Start or join a Zoom meeting.

2. Navigate to the **React** icon on the **Meeting Control** bar and click on it:

Figure 3.12: React icon

3.   A window with available reactions will appear:

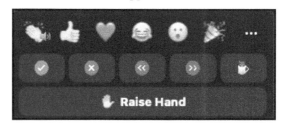

Figure 3.13: Available reactions

4.   Now choose which reaction you would like to use by clicking on it. The reaction will appear in your camera's video panel in the top-left corner. All participants in the meeting will be able to see your reaction.

5.   The top six default reactions are also animated, and the participants will be able to view the animation from their video gallery in their panel. These will be displayed for 10 seconds, then disappear.

*   Clapping hands (this reaction will also play an audio clap sound)

*   Thumbs up

*   Heart

*   Tears of joy

*   Open mouth

*   Party popper (tada, celebration)

Figure 3.14: Animated reactions

The bottom six reactions are static. They have no animation and will stay on the screen until manually turned off. To turn off a static reaction, just click on the reaction a second time. An example of when to use these might be when you want to ask your meeting attendees a question and you want a non-verbal "Yes" or "No" for everyone to see.

- Yes

- No

- Slow down

- Speed up

- I'm away

- Raise hand/lower hand

6. You can also use additional emojis by clicking ...:

Figure 3.15: Emojis

7. Notice the ^ to the right of the **React** icon. This gives you additional options:

Figure 3.16: Additional options

- **Play chime for raised hands**: If you click the **Raise Hand** reaction, the host will hear a chime, giving them audio feedback that someone has a question or comment.

- **Recognize hand gestures**: If a participant physically holds up their hand for a question or thumbs up, Zoom will recognize this gesture and automatically place the reaction in their video panel:

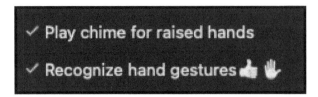

Figure 3.17: Animated reactions

You should now be a marvel at using reactions in your next Zoom meeting!

Using meeting chat

Using your camera and mic for video and audio during a Zoom meeting is the cornerstone way to interact with meeting participants. Sharing content via a desktop or application is also a pillar of what Zoom can do. Creating whiteboards and Notes are both ways in which meeting participants can create, collaborate, and share. But sometimes, chat is the most effective way to communicate with meeting attendees before, during, or after a meeting. There are two chat methods. We will be discussing both methods in this recipe.

In-meeting chat

This chat method is only available during a meeting. This is a great option for meetings that will only happen once, or for impromptu, ad-hoc meetings that aren't scheduled. When the meeting is over, the chat feature will end.

How to do it...

1. Start or join a Zoom meeting.

2. Navigate to the **Chat** icon on the *Meeting Control* bar and click on it:

Figure 3.18: Chat icon

3. A chat window will open to the right of your Zoom meeting screen:

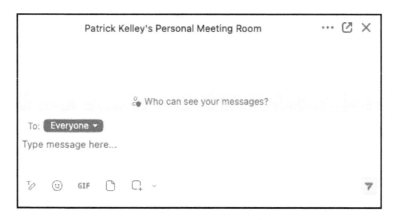

Figure 3.19: Chat window

4. You can immediately begin chatting with meeting participants by typing in your message and hitting the **send** button. If configured, you will have the choice to send messages to Everyone or to send Private Messages to meeting participants.

5. There are a lot of different options to increase your collaboration effectiveness as well. Use the bottom toolbar icons to turn these on:

   • Rich Text Mode – Enable advanced font features such as bold, italics, numbers, and bullets

   • Emojis – Send emojis in the meeting chat

   • GIFs – Search for and use GIFs as reactions

   • File attachments – Upload files into the meeting chat

   • Screenshots – Capture screenshots from your desktop to send in the chat

Figure 3.20: Chat features

6. Attendees will receive notifications of new chats sent during the meeting. In this example, there are four chats that haven't been read:

Figure 3.21: Chat notifications

7. On the top of your chat window, notice the **....** Click on the ellipses to gain access to chat permission control.

8. As a host, you can control who can chat and save the chat:

   • **Save Chat** – Save the text portion of the chat locally to your computer. No attachments, GIFs, or screenshots will be saved.

   • **No one** – Chat is disabled during the meeting.

   • **Hosts and co-hosts** – Only the host and co-host of a meeting can chat.

   • **Everyone** – Everyone can chat, and all chats are seen by all meeting attendees.

   • **Everyone and anyone directly** – This is the same as the **Everyone** option, but in addition, users can send direct messages to other meeting participants that will stay private between them.

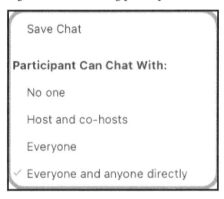

Figure 3.22: Chat permissions

You've now mastered how to chat in a Zoom meeting. You are really getting the hang of this!

Continuous Meeting Chat

This method can only be used with scheduled and reoccurring meetings. This feature allows meeting participants to chat before, during, and after a meeting by creating a dedicated group chat in Zoom Team Chat for all meeting participants. This is the preferred method for meetings for continuous projects that involve much collaboration between meeting participants. This is ideal when users wish to communicate and continue to chat about the subject or topic beyond just during the actual meeting.

How to do it...

1. **Schedule** a new Zoom meeting. You learned how to do this in a previous recipe (*Schedule a Zoom meeting*).

2. By default, **Enable Continuous Meeting Chat** is toggled on:

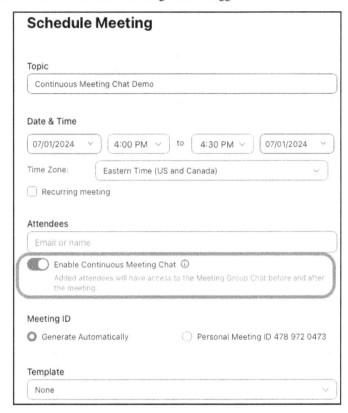

Figure 3.23: Enable Chat

3. Once you have gone through scheduling a meeting, a new Zoom Team Meeting chat space will be created. Notice that in step 2, I named the meeting Continuous Meeting Chat Demo. This will also be the name of the Zoom Team Chat space:

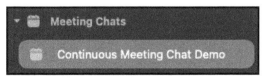

Figure 3.24: Meeting Chat

4. Any meeting attendee within the same organization can start chatting with other meeting invitees. This feature will be available before, during, and after the meeting.

5. To begin chatting, there are three methods you can use:

    • Calendar Panel: Navigate to your meeting invitation and click **…**, then choose **Chat**:

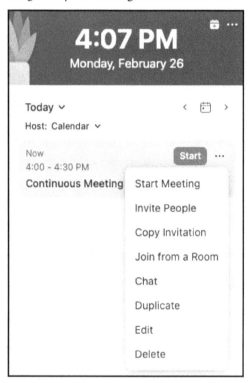

Figure 3.25: Chat from Calendar Panel

    • Zoom Calendar: Navigate to the meeting on your Zoom Calendar. Right-click the meeting and choose **Chat**:

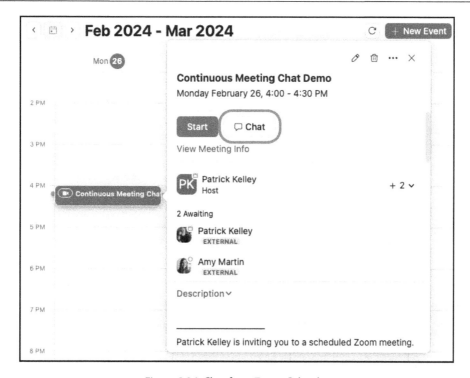

Figure 3.26: Chat from Zoom Calendar

- Zoom Team Chat: Navigate to the Meeting Chat in Team Chat, as in Figure 3.18.

6. Before, during, or after a meeting, you can use Team Chat to chat with meeting attendees invited to the meeting. During the meeting, you can also use the Chat feature from your Zoom meeting. All chats, files, attachments, screenshots, and so on will be saved persistently in the Meeting Chat channel. Meeting participants will be able to asynchronously view and collaborate via Continuous Meeting Chat.

There's more...

By default, only meeting attendees internal to your organization are invited to Continuous Meeting Chat for security reasons. An external chat invitee can send a request to the meeting organizer to join the Meeting Chat. Once approved, the external attendee can view, create, and collaborate using Team Chat.

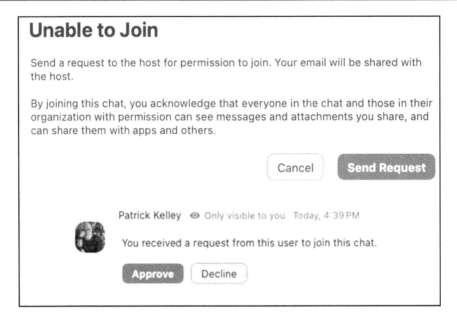

Figure 3.27: External Meeting Chat request

We will dive deeper into Zoom Team Chat in *Chapter 5* for greater depth and clarity regarding all the Team Chat features.

You are now a complete wizard with Meeting Chat in Zoom!

Using annotations

Annotations are a great way to highlight content shared during a meeting. Zoom allows users to annotate and collaborate in real time with desktops, applications, and really any item that is shared during a meeting. This in-meeting product allows remote participants to easily brainstorm on content. Not only can the presenter utilize this powerful tool during a meeting, but so too can attendees for an immersive and effective way to give feedback during a presentation. Zoom provides an assortment of annotation tools.

How to do it...

1. Start or join a Zoom meeting.

2. **Share** any content during a meeting such as a desktop, application, or whiteboard. Annotating works with all of them.

3. Notice on the **Meeting Control** bar that there is an **Annotate** icon. Click on it to open a new Annotation toolbar. By default, this will appear to the left of your screenshare. You can click and hold your left mouse button and drag this toolbar anywhere on your screen:

Figure 3.28: Annotation toolbar

4. The toolbar contains many options to annotate on the screenshare window for hosts and participants. Descriptions of the icons in the toolbar from left to right are as follows:

- **Mouse**: Deactivate annotation tools and switch to your mouse pointer. This button is blue if annotation tools are deactivated.

- **Select** (only available if you started the shared screen or whiteboard): Select, move, or resize your annotations. To select several annotations at once, click and drag your mouse to display a selection area.

- **Text**: Insert text.

- **Draw**: Insert lines, arrows, shapes, and *Vanishing Pen* and *Smart Pen* features:

  - **Vanishing Pen**: Allow the presenter to annotate on the whiteboard or shared screen without having to erase or undo their last addition, as the annotation will fade away within a couple of seconds. (My favorite tool!)

  - **Smart Pen**: Draw a shape such as a circle or square. Zoom will automatically fix it to have the perfect dimensions.

- **Stamp**: Insert a predefined icon such as a checkmark or star.

- **Spotlight** (only available if you started the shared screen or whiteboard): Display your mouse pointer to all participants as a laser pointer when your mouse is within the area being shared. Use this to point out parts of the screen to other participants.

- **Eraser**: Click and drag to erase parts of your annotation.

- **Color**: Change the formatting color of your annotations.

- **Undo**: Undo your latest annotation.

- **Redo**: Redo the latest annotation that you undid.

- **Clear**: Delete all annotations.

- **Save**: Save the shared screen/whiteboard and annotations as a PNG or PDF.

- **Dock toolbar**: Statically stick the toolbar to the top center of your shared screen.

- **Share**: Display who can save and share your annotations.

- **Close**: Close the Annotation toolbar.

5. In the following figure, I have used several tools from the Annotation toolbar to collaborate with meeting attendees on an example Excel spreadsheet:

    *   I used the draw tool to circle the word **Summary** in red

    *   I used the stamp tool to approve all the **Budget** expenses with a green check and to place hearts next to all the income amounts

    *   I used the draw tool to point a red arrow at **Monthly Income**

    *   I used the shape tool to create a red rectangle

    *   I used the text tool to create white text saying **Love it!**

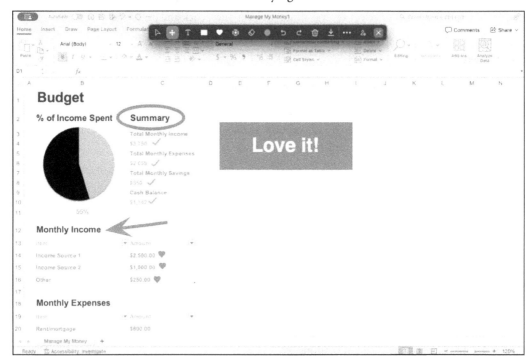

Figure 3.29: Annotation example

6. If you click on **... More** in your **Meeting Control** bar, you can also click **Disable Annotations for Others** should you wish to not have attendees annotate your presentation. By default, annotation is open to everyone in the meeting.

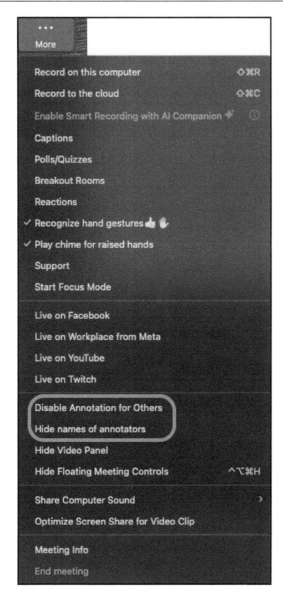

Figure 3.30: Zoom settings

7. The possibilities are endless. Use your imagination to collaborate on screenshares with your meeting participants.

Using the meeting timers

The thing that annoys meeting attendees the most is when meetings run long and make them late for their next meeting. Don't be that person who doesn't keep track of time. Zoom can help! Meeting timers keep you on track with meeting duration. Learn how to use these vital tools next.

Getting ready

1. Make sure **Meeting timers** are enabled. Navigate to the top-right corner of your Zoom client. Click the profile icon and choose **Settings**:

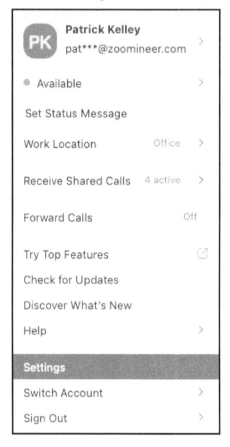

Figure 3.31: Zoom settings

2. Click **General** on the left-hand tab, then verify that **Show meeting timers** is checked:

Figure 3.32: Show meeting timers

How to do it...

1. Start or join a Zoom meeting.

2. Look at the top-right corner of your meeting screen. Notice the timer:

Figure 3.33: Meeting timer

3. This is a duration timer for your Zoom meeting. This indicates how long you've been in the meeting.

4. More importantly, if you've scheduled a meeting, click **V** to the right of the meeting timer and select **Time Remaining**:

Figure 3.34: Time Remaining

5. **Time Remaining** now counts down the time you've scheduled for the meeting. As a meeting organizer, maintain vigilance on this timer.

6. When your meeting has less than five minutes remaining, the timer turns yellow. This warns you, as a meeting host, that the meeting is about to end:

Figure 3.35: Less than five minutes remaining

7. Be cognizant of meeting attendees' time. It's vital. Be sure to wrap up action items and next steps during the final five minutes of your meeting!

I think you've become an amazing meeting time organizer now! Applause…

Using the mute feature for audio and video

Zoom meetings are built on sharing audio and video, but there are times when you may need to mute audio or video or both. It's always best practice to enable video during any Zoom meeting. No one loves presenting to a bunch of black gallery boxes. The whole point of a video meeting is to see attendees' reactions and non-verbal feedback. If you were in a conference room watching a presentation, you would need to be present and paying attention. It's the same with a Zoom meeting. With that said, there are times when you may wish to mute your video camera feed as well as audio during a meeting. For example, I just had surgery on my eyes and my face was in bandages. I'm pretty sure no one wanted to see my video, so I muted it during meetings. The same is true with audio. If my dog is barking at the mailman or my child asks me to read them a book during a meeting, I'm pretty sure no one in the meeting wants to hear that. The point is that Zoom created the ability to mute audio and video for a reason. Let's learn how to do that with a few options.

How to do it...

1. Start or join a Zoom meeting.

2. Notice that on the **Meeting Control** bar, there are microphone and camera icons. These are your audio and video controls:

Figure 3.36: Audio and video controls

3. If you hover over each of the icons, you have the ability to mute both audio and video by clicking the corresponding icons. Once you mute either option, a red dash appears over the top:

Figure 3.37: Mute function

4. If you are a meeting attendee and watching the host of the meeting present, it's best practice to mute your audio and leave your video on. This helps stop audio distractions from being shared with all participants. Remember, be present during your meetings. Non-verbal feedback during a presentation is awesome to see from all attendees during a meeting. You can easily come off mute by clicking your microphone icon to share your audio.

> **Note**
> Zoom has created a shortcut key to temporarily unmute your audio during a meeting. Press and hold the space bar at any time to unmute your audio. This is helpful when you may have feedback you wish to share during the meeting.

5. As mentioned already, sharing your video in most circumstances is ideal. Of course, there are times when you may wish to mute your video feed. For example, there are times during a meeting when my dog loves to come and say hello and jump on my lap as I work remotely. I don't imagine most attendees want to see my French Bulldog licking my face during a meeting. Therefore, I will mute my video to not cause a distraction by clicking **Stop Video** during my Zoom meeting.

> **Note**
> Using Zoom Avatars is another great way to mute your video during a meeting. We will dive more into this feature in *Chapter 8*.

You've now learned how to properly use the mute feature. You are amazing!

Using Zoom virtual backgrounds

What's behind your camera video matters. That's why Zoom created virtual backgrounds. It's an amazing way to add depth of field, branding, and creativity to your next Zoom meeting. We don't always have the ability to join meetings from a Hollywood backdrop. Sometimes, we are on our laptops in an airport, but still need to present during a meeting with a sense of professionalism. Virtual backgrounds from Zoom allow you as a meeting presenter or attendee to utilize this feature to brand a customer presentation or create an immersive and imaginative thought or idea during a meeting.

How to do it...

1. Start or join a Zoom meeting.
2. Navigate to the **Video** icon on your **Meeting Control** bar.
3. Click the ^ to the right of your video icon:

Figure 3.38: Video options

4. Next, click **Choose Virtual Background…**:

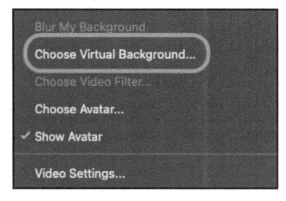

Figure 3.39: Choose Virtual Background

5. A virtual background window will open. Zoom has a few virtual backgrounds to choose from already in the client. Images as well as videos can be used. Click on any one to apply it to your video panel. It will be highlighted in blue once the virtual background is selected and applied:

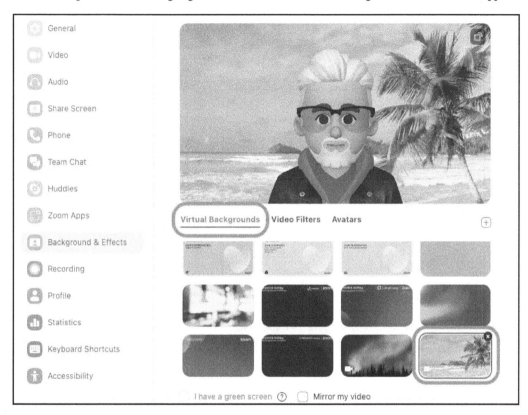

Figure 3.40: Choose Virtual Background

6. Zoom has a full library of available virtual backgrounds that you can download and add to your client (https://www.zoom.com/en/products/virtual-meetings/features/virtual-background-library/).

7. To add any virtual background, just click the + icon in the virtual background window. A browser window will open. Navigate to the virtual background you wish to add.

There's more...

1. You can also search the web for literally thousands of different backgrounds.

2. You can also design your own background with graphics applications such as Microsoft PowerPoint, Google Slides, or Canva. Be as creative as you want.

Here are some guidelines to keep in mind when using or creating virtual backgrounds:

- Compatible formats include GIF, JPG, JPEG, and PNG files. Zoom recommends an image with a 16:9 aspect ratio and a minimum resolution of 1280x720 pixels.

- Videos should be MP4 or MOV files with a minimum resolution of 480x360 pixels (360p) and a maximum resolution of 1920x1020 pixels (1080p).

3.   The use of a green screen is optional. To enable this feature, check **I have a green screen**:

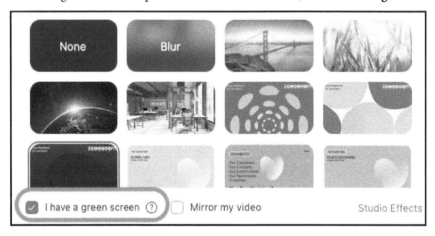

Figure 3.41: Green screen

4.   Using a green screen provides the best virtual background effect and uses fewer system resources during the meeting. This requires you to have a solid-colored screen, curtain, or wall behind you, which Zoom will replace with the selected virtual background. This improves sharpness and definition around your face, head, ears, and hair. This isn't required by any means but does improve quality.

You should now be a professional virtual backgrounder!

4
Zoom Phone

Zoom Phone is a comprehensive cloud-based communication solution that integrates seamlessly with the Zoom platform, offering businesses a unified communications experience. With Zoom Phone, users can make and receive calls, send text messages, and hold video meetings all from a single application, enhancing productivity and collaboration within organizations.

One of the key features of Zoom Phone is its simplicity and ease of use. The interface is intuitive, making it easy for users to navigate and access the various communication tools available. Whether making a call, scheduling a meeting, or sending a message, everything can be done with just a few clicks, streamlining communication workflows and saving valuable time.

Another notable aspect of Zoom Phone is its reliability and call quality. Built on Zoom's robust infrastructure, Zoom Phone offers crystal-clear voice quality and ensures that calls are stable and uninterrupted, even in low-bandwidth environments. This reliability is crucial for businesses, where communication downtime can result in lost opportunities and decreased productivity.

Integration with the wider Zoom ecosystem is another strength of Zoom Phone. Users can seamlessly transition between voice calls, video meetings, and chat conversations, creating a unified communication experience across various channels.

Security and privacy are top priorities for Zoom Phone. The platform incorporates end-to-end encryption for calls, ensuring that sensitive information remains protected from unauthorized access.

Zoom Phone is a powerful communication solution that offers simplicity, reliability, integration, security, and scalability. By providing a unified communication experience, Zoom Phone empowers businesses to enhance collaboration, increase productivity, and drive success in today's fast-paced digital world.

In this chapter, we're going to cover the following main recipes:

- Purchasing Zoom Phone
- Making a Zoom Phone call
- Using calling features
- Setting up calling handling

- Setting up phone greetings

- Using SMS messaging

- Using call recording

- Setting up emergency calling

- Using Phone Assistant

- Using call transcription

- Technical requirements

As a best practice, always update your Zoom to the latest version. Refer to the *Technical requirements* section of *Chapter 2* for a refresher on how to do it.

Purchasing Zoom Phone

Zoom Phone is an add-on component in addition to the Zoom core offering. If you are a business, this can be purchased with a *Business Plus* or *Enterprise* license. Pricing is available directly from Zoom here: `https://zoom.us/pricing`.

An individual or smaller company can certainly purchase *Business Plus* or *Enterprise* licenses directly from Zoom that include Zoom Phone; however, users can also purchase individual phone plans here: `https://zoom.us/pricing/zoom-phone`.

Contact Zoom sales directly for any licensing questions.

> **Note**
> Zoom Phone administration and setup are outside the scope of this book. This cookbook is a user's guide and has recipes that focus on the workflows and features of the Zoom platform. So, let's assume your Zoom Phone system has already been set up and configured for end users, and you want to jump into how to use the Zoom Phone product.

Making a Zoom Phone call

Once you have been assigned a new Zoom Phone license and phone number, you will see an additional icon in your Zoom client's top navigation bar. We will start there to access all phone-related features. Making a phone call is obviously the most important feature to learn. Let's jump in.

How to do it...

Navigate to the phone icon on your top navigation bar and click on **Phone**.

Figure 4.1 – Zoom Phone

Enter the phone number or name of a person you want to dial. You can use your keyboard to enter numbers, copy and paste, or simply enter them from the number pad in the client.

Figure 4.2 – Enter name/number on Zoom Phone

Once you have entered the phone number you wish to dial, click the blue phone icon to place a call.

Using Zoom calling features

After a Zoom Phone call has connected, additional features are available that can assist you in handling your live phone calls. Let's walk through these features in greater detail.

How to do it...

Once your call has connected, the Zoom Phone window will change to additional features that are available to use during the call.

Click on any feature pictured in the following figure to utilize during your live call:

Figure 4.3 – Zoom Phone features

- **Mute**: Click to mute and unmute the phone call.
- **Keypad**: Use to enter DTMF commands during a call.

- **Audio**: Use this to change which devices are used during the call, such as a speaker and microphone.

- **Add call**: Use this to add additional people to make your phone call a conferencing call.

- **Hold**: Places the current call on hold.

- **Transfer**: Allows you to transfer the current call to another device or number.

- **Record**: Record your PSTN call (users will be notified when this feature is turned on).

- **Meet**: Escalate the Zoom Phone call to a full Zoom meeting.

- **Park**: Place a call on hold. Resume the call from another user or phone.

You now know the basic functions of a Zoom Phone call!

Setting up call-handling features

There are times when you may want to have more than just your Zoom Phone ring at the same time for incoming calls, such as a separate physical phone or even your mobile device. For example, I have a PSTN line in my garage, as I don't want to miss an important Zoom phone call. I have my Zoom Phone set up to simultaneously ring my garage phone. This may be beneficial if you sometimes work in a remote office with a separate line, and you want your Zoom client to not only ring on your desktop and mobile but also at your remote work location. There may be times when you want to forward a call to a separate work extension or even an external contact. There are many scenarios that you might have that need additional call handling. Let's dive into how to set them up.

How to do it...

1. Go to your Zoom portal from any browser: `https://zoom.us/account`.
2. Sign in to the portal with your Zoom credentials.

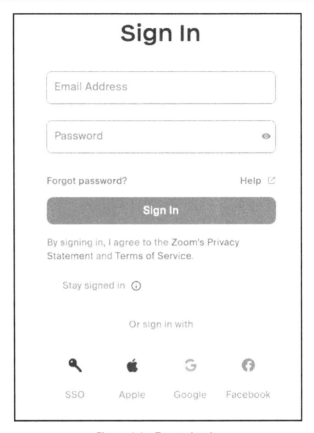

Figure 4.4 – Zoom sign-in

3. Navigate to the **Phone** tab on the left navigation bar and click it. Then, navigate to **Settings** on the top tab. Both will be highlighted in blue.

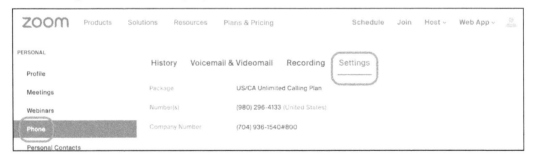

Figure 4.5 – Zoom Phone settings

4. Scroll down until you see **Call Handling**.

5. In this section of the admin portal, you can control all call-handling features of your Zoom Phone.

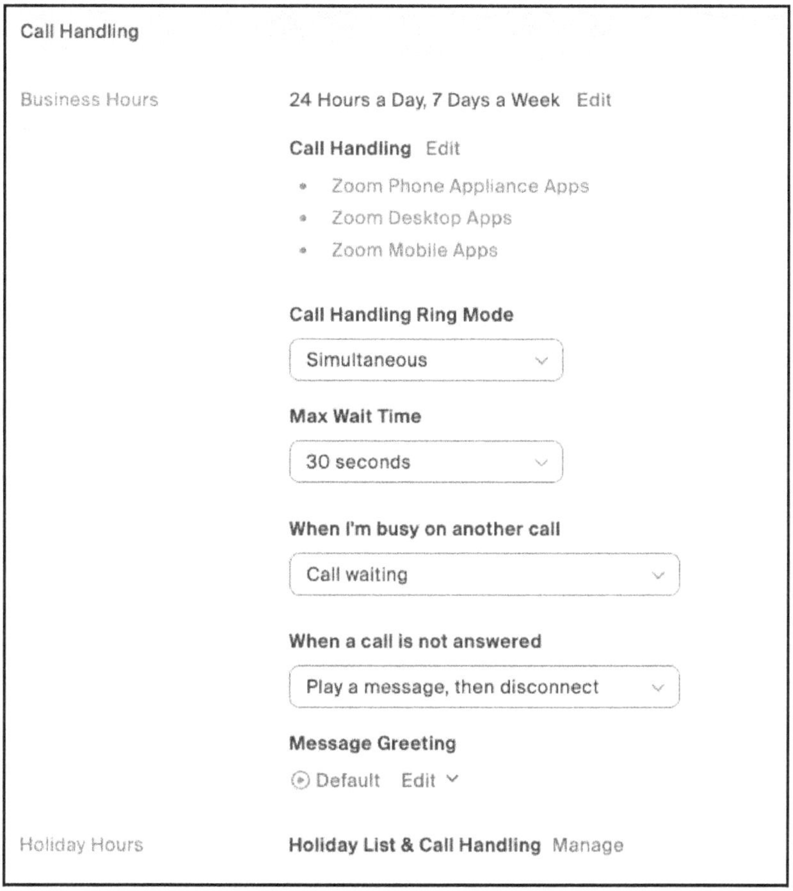

```
Call Handling

Business Hours          24 Hours a Day, 7 Days a Week   Edit

                        Call Handling   Edit
                          •   Zoom Phone Appliance Apps
                          •   Zoom Desktop Apps
                          •   Zoom Mobile Apps

                        Call Handling Ring Mode
                        ┌─────────────────────────────────┐
                        │  Simultaneous            ∨       │
                        └─────────────────────────────────┘
                        Max Wait Time
                        ┌─────────────────────────────────┐
                        │  30 seconds              ∨       │
                        └─────────────────────────────────┘

                        When I'm busy on another call
                        ┌───────────────────────────────────────┐
                        │  Call waiting                    ∨      │
                        └───────────────────────────────────────┘

                        When a call is not answered
                        ┌───────────────────────────────────────┐
                        │  Play a message, then disconnect  ∨     │
                        └───────────────────────────────────────┘

                        Message Greeting
                        ⊙ Default   Edit ∨

Holiday Hours           Holiday List & Call Handling   Manage
```

Figure 4.6 – Call Handling

There are multiple areas to enable additional call-handling capabilities of Zoom Phone. Let's review each of these features:

- **Business Hours**: These are the times when you wish to enable additional phone handling capabilities. By default, this is set to 24/7 (basically, always on). If you wish to have separate call-handling rules when open or closed, set your business hours here, and a **Closed Hours** section will be added to **Call Handling**.

- **Call Handling**: This controls which applications you want controlled via the **Call Handling** settings. By default, **Zoom Phone Appliance Apps** (physical Zoom phones), **Zoom Desktop Apps**, and **Zoom Mobile Apps** are selected. This means that all three apps will ring during an incoming call. Should you wish to change these settings, click **Edit**. This will allow you to toggle on/off the apps that ring, as well as add additional external contacts or external phone numbers to simultaneously ring during an incoming call.

- **Call Handling Ring Mode**: **Simultaneous** is on by default. This means that all the apps and phone numbers you have in the **Call Handling** section ring at the same time. This can be toggled to **Sequential**. This will then ring each device in the sequential order listed in **Call Handling**, until the call reaches a max time or is not answered (more on that shortly).

- **Max Wait Time**: This is the amount of time devices will ring before going on to the next layer of call handling. For example, if **Call Handling Ring Mode** were set to **Sequential**, the Zoom Phone appliance would ring for 30 seconds, Zoom desktop apps would ring for 30 seconds, and so on. This is 30 seconds by default. Click the drop-down menu to change the duration.

- **When I'm busy on another call**: If you are currently on a Zoom Phone call, this is the call-handling procedure a caller will encounter. You can click the drop-down menu to handle busy calls:

- **Call Waiting**: Alerts you of another call coming in and allows you to place the current call on hold and answer it.

- **Forward to voicemail/videomail**: Forward the caller to a voice or videomail greeting. (Videomail is a Zoom Phone-only option when receiving a phone call from another Zoom Phone account. This option will be covered in the following recipe.)

- **Play a message, then disconnect**: Plays a default message or a custom message (covered in another recipe) when receiving another call during a live Zoom phone call. The **Message Greeting** option appears when this is chosen.

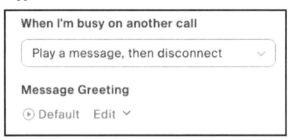

Figure 4.7 – Playing a message greeting

- **Play a busy signal**: When on a phone call and another phone call is received, the calling party will receive a busy signal.

- **Forward to another extension**: During a phone call, the calling party is forwarded to another extension.

- **Forward to External Contacts**: If you are on a phone call, the calling party is forwarded to an external contact's phone outside the organization.

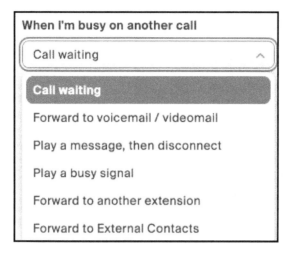

Figure 4.8 – When on another call

- **When a call is not answered**: Much like the previous option, you can choose what to do with received phone calls that aren't answered:

- **Forward to voicemail/videomail**: Forwards the caller to a voice or videomail greeting. (Videomail is a Zoom Phone-only option when receiving a phone call from another Zoom Phone account.).

- **Play a message, then disconnect**: Plays a default or custom message when receiving another call during a live Zoom phone call. The **Message Greeting** option appears when this is chosen.

- **Disconnect**: Completely drops the phone call of the calling party with no option to leave a message (which is harsh, so don't use this one!).

- **Forward to another extension**: After the max wait time of the call, the unanswered call is sent to another extension in the organization.

- **Forward to External Contacts**: If unanswered, the calling party is forwarded to an external contact's phone number outside the organization.

- **Holiday Hours**: Much like **Business Hours**, **Holidays Hours** can be customized to your specific business or region. Click the **Manage** link to set up custom holiday hours. A separate window will appear, allowing you to enter specific dates and times of your holiday for call handling. You can even set up a custom holiday greeting. In *Figure 4.9*, I set up a New Year's holiday call-handling example.

Figure 4.9 – Holiday List & Call Handling

You've become a Jedi master at Zoom Phone Call handling. May the force be with you!

Setting up phone greetings

There are two main greetings in Zoom Phone – Zoom voicemail and videomail. Both offer a convenient solution to manage missed calls and ensure seamless communication. When users are unable to answer a call, Zoom voicemail or videomail steps in, allowing callers to leave messages that can be accessed later. With features such as personalized greetings and message forwarding, users can customize their greetings experience to suit their needs. This not only helps maintain professionalism but also ensures that important messages are never missed. Whether in the office or on the go, Zoom greetings keep users connected and informed, enhancing productivity and efficiency in communication workflows.

Voicemail

Zoom Voicemail can be used for missed calls, allowing the person who called to leave a voice message that can then be listened to later. Voicemail also has a transcription that allows you to read the voicemail should you need to quickly scan what the message is about, without listening to the whole message.

How to do it...

1. Navigate to **Call Handling** using *steps 1* to *4* of the *Setting up phone greetings* recipe.

2. Navigate to **When I'm busy on another call** and **When a call is not answered**, respectively. Click the drop-down option and select **Forward to voicemail / videomail** for each, as illustrated in the following figure.

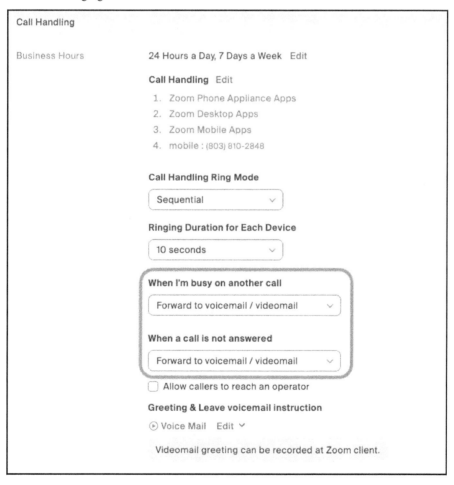

Figure 4.10 – Voicemail/videomail

3.   A new option will appear beneath that says **Greeting & Leave voicemail instruction**. By default, a generic greeting will play. If you wish to customize this greeting, click **Edit**, and then select **Add Audio**.

There are three choices to add audio to your voicemail:

- **Text to Speech**: This option allows you to type in what you wish your greeting to play, and a voice will narrate the text as speech for you. You can pick a language as well as choose from different voices.

- **Upload**: This allows you to upload a prerecorded file less than 10 MB (a WAV or MP3) to play as your voicemail recording.

- **Record by Computer**: You can directly record your own voice, leaving a message to use as a greeting to users.

Once you have selected a greeting type, your voicemail will be activated. You can click the play icon next to **Voice Mail** to listen to what your greeting sounds like to callers.

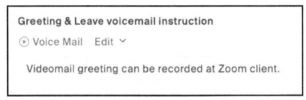

Figure 4.11 – Voicemail

That's it! You've successfully set up voicemail in Zoom Phone.

Videomail

Zoom Phone users can record a video greeting that is played for missed inbound calls from other Zoom Phone users in their organization. These users can then leave a videomail message that can be replayed.

How to do it...

1.   From your Zoom client, click on your profile picture, and then click **Settings**.

2.   Click the **Phone** tab.

3.   Scroll down to the **Video Greeting** section.

Video Greeting:	Internal Zoom Phone callers will see this video greeting and external callers will hear your voice greeting
	Record

Figure 4.12 – Video Greeting

4. Click the **Record** link.

5. A separate recording window will appear. Click the record icon to record your video greeting for missed calls.

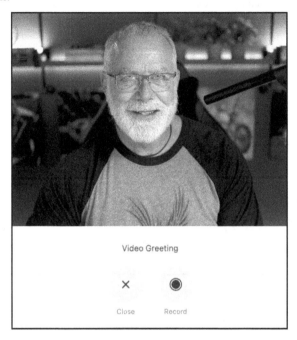

Figure 4.13 – Recording a video greeting

6. Record your videomail greeting. If you are happy with it, click **Done**. If you need to do a retake, hit the **Retake** icon.

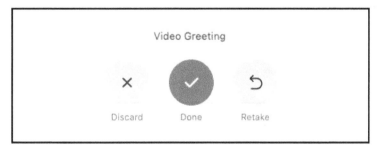

Figure 4.14 – Video Greeting

7. You are a champ. All your greetings are now set up in Zoom Phone!

Using SMS

Zoom Phone SMS allows you to send and receive text messages (SMS) using the Zoom desktop client, mobile app, or Zoom web app. This is a powerful way to use SMS from your Zoom client as an additional way to communicate.

How to do it...

1. Go to the top navigation bar in your Zoom client and click **Phone**.

Figure 4.15 – Zoom Phone

2. The **Phone** window will open. Navigate to the **SMS** tab.

Figure 4.16 – The SMS tab

3. To send a new SMS message, click the new SMS icon.

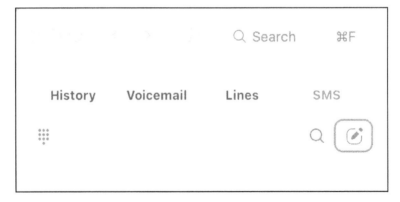

Figure 4.17 – The new SMS icon

4. A new SMS window will appear to the right. Enter a name or phone number or even multiple names/numbers in the **To:** field.

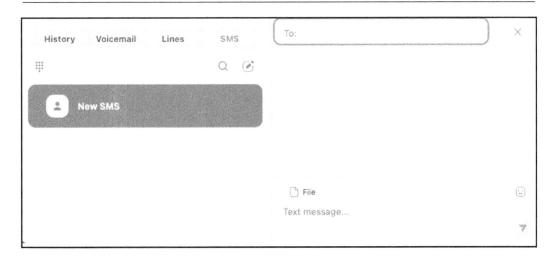

Figure 4.18 – The To: field

5.   Type your message in the **Text message…** field. You can certainly use text in this field, but you can also attach files and use emojis – for example, pictures, PDFs, and even documents such as Microsoft Word and Excel files.

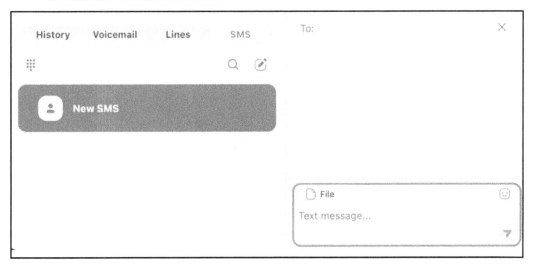

Figure 4.19 – Text message…

6.   Once you've compiled your message, hit the send arrow.

Figure 4.20 – Sending an SMS message

7.   As you can see in the following figure, I sent myself a text to my iPhone. Then, I sent a picture followed by a heart emoji.

Figure 4.21 – A text message example

8. Just like chat, calls, and meetings, you will be notified when a new SMS message arrives with a red bubble notification in the Phone icon, in the top navigation bar in your Zoom client.

You're done! You now know how to harness the power of Zoom Phone and SMS.

Recording a Zoom Phone call

At times, it might be necessary to record a call. For example, it might be an important business call from your mobile and you aren't able to take notes, or you might work in an industry that has compliance regulations that all calls need to be recorded. Whatever the reason, this can be done using Zoom Phone's call recording feature.

How to do it...

Make a phone call with Zoom Phone. Once connected, the call options window will appear. Click the **Record** icon to begin recording the call. A message will be played, informing all participants in the call that the call is being recorded: "*This call is being recorded. Please press 1 to provide your consent to be recorded.*"

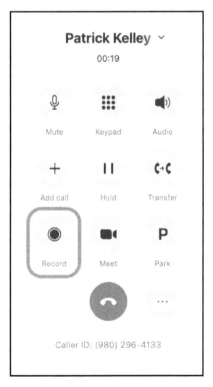

Figure 4.22 – Recording a call

After the call has been completed, you will be able to listen to any recorded call from your **History** tab by clicking **Play Recording**. Any call that has been recorded will have a record icon underneath the phone number.

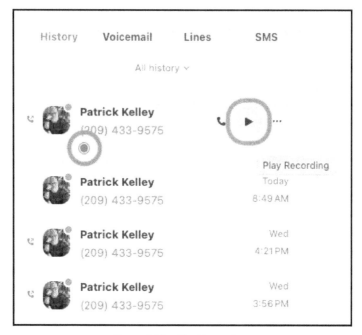

Figure 4.23 – Play Recording

You can also sort all calls that have been recorded from the **History** tab. Choose **Recording** from the drop-down menu. All calls that have a recording will be listed in chronological order.

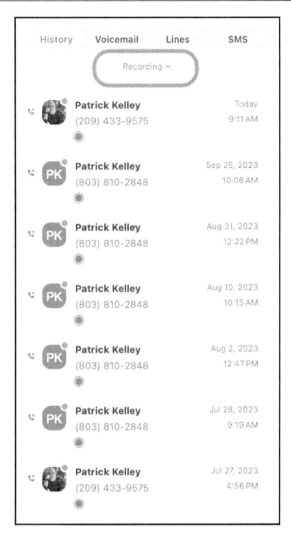

Figure 4.24 – Recorded Calls

You have now mastered how to use the **Record** feature in Zoom Phone!

Setting up emergency calling

Your emergency address is the address that emergency services will respond to in the event you have dialed an emergency number, such as 911. In the event of an emergency call, your address can be shared with a public-safety answering point, such as a 911 dispatch center.

Nomadic emergency services enable Zoom to assist in determining your location, and emergency calling should be used only for the purposes of responding to your emergency calls. You will need to set up your location for this feature to work properly.

How to do it...

1. From your Zoom client, go to **Settings**, and then click the **Phone** tab.

2. Scroll down until you see **Location Permission**. Enable this to allow Zoom to have additional access to your location for emergency calls. This enables advanced features such as location-based access and call routing.

3. Below **Location Permissions** is your emergency address. You may already have one detected by Zoom. If this is the correct address of your current location, you don't need to do anything. If this is blank or you need to update the address, click the **Personal Location or Address** link.

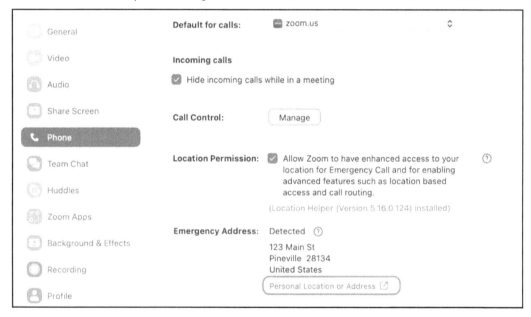

Figure 4.25 – An emergency call address

4. The Zoom portal browser will open. Click the **Add** button to enter a new address.

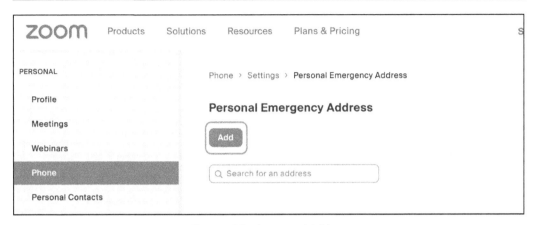

Figure 4.26 – A personal Address

5. Add the address of the location you want to set for emergency services, and then click **Save**.

6. From the Zoom portal, you can now choose which address you would like as your emergency address. Again, that location is **Phone | Settings | Emergency Address**.

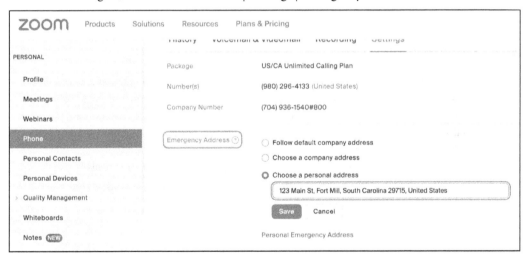

Figure 4.27 – Emergency Address

7. Choose which address applies to your current address. By default, the company address will be picked. This assumes you may be working from a corporate office or a location that is assigned. But if you are working from home or traveling and wish to pick a personal location, this is an option as well, as shown in the last radio button choice in *Figure 4.27*. I added a fictitious address in *step 5* and then chose that as my emergency address from my personal choices. Once your address is chosen, click **Save**.

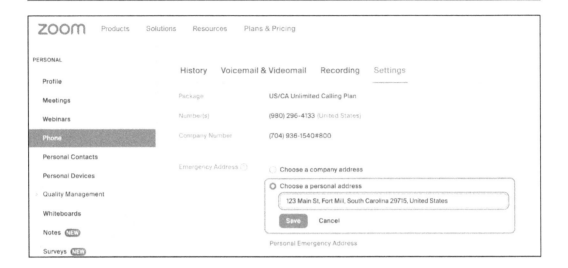

Figure 4.28 – A personal address

8. You're all set. You now know how to apply emergency calling.

Using Phone Assistant

You can certainly use the full Zoom client to place and receive calls, but Zoom includes a Zoom Phone Assistant tool as well. This is a small form-factor phone client that includes most of the functionality of Zoom Phone, just in a widget-type application. This allows you to stay focused on a particular application without having the bigger screen real estate of the Zoom Phone client take over. For example, I might be on a call discussing the details of a large spreadsheet. I want to use my full screen for my Excel file and not have the Zoom Phone client taking over the desktop. I can easily use Zoom Phone Assistant and move it out of the way but still have most of my call functionality easily available.

How to do it...

1. From your Zoom client, go to **Settings**, and then make sure you are in the **General** tab.

2. Scroll down until you see the **Zoom Assistant** tab. Toggle in on.

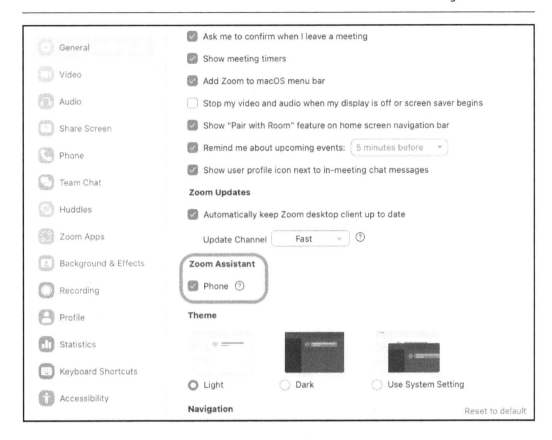

Figure 4.29 – The Zoom Assistant toggle

3. Now, your Zoom Phone Assistant tool will be available on your screen. Note that at the bottom, there are dial pad, call history, and voicemail icons. Click on any of them to quickly navigate to these areas in Zoom Phone.

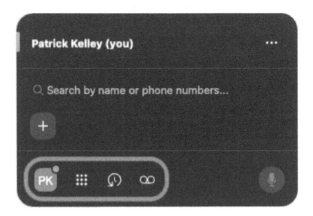

Figure 4.30 – Zoom Phone Assistant

4.   You can click and drag the app anywhere on your screen. You can also drag Phone Assistant to the far right, left, or bottom edges of your desktop, and it will dock itself behind the screen. This means just a small sliver of the app appears, taking just a small fraction of screen real estate. Then, when you want to use the app, just hover over it with your mouse, and it will slide out. It will also slide out when receiving a call to notify you of an incoming call.

5.   Once you place or receive a call, multiple in-call options appear in the app, such as call recording, call park, call transfer, call information, and call hold.

Figure 4.31 – The Zoom Phone Assistant options

6. During a call, a duration timer and mute button also appear.

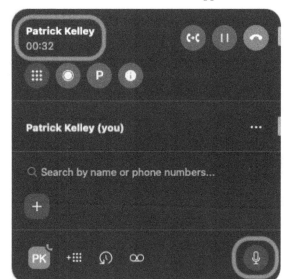

Figure 4.32 – A call duration timer and mute button

7. That's it! You can now start using Zoom Phone Assistant.

Call Transcription

During a real-time Zoom Phone call, you can also have live Call Transcription. When enabled, the phone call audio is converted into a text caption for a better understanding of what is being said. For example, in a loud environment, it may be difficult to hear the call participants audio over your headset or laptop's speakers. The audio from all participants is captioned with their names and a timestamp, but they are only visible to you. During the call, you can scroll back to view captions rendered earlier in the conversation. Each time a transcription is turned on or off during the call, the participants on the call will hear or see a notice that this setting has been enabled or disabled.

How to do it...

1. From the Zoom client, click on your picture profile or initials, choose **Settings**, and then navigate to **Phone**.

2. Scroll down until you see **Live transcript settings**, and tick the checkbox.

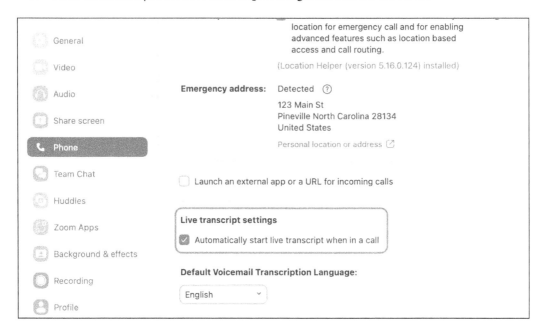

Figure 4.33 – Live transcript settings

3. Now, when you place or receive a Zoom Phone call, a transcription window will appear to the right of your phone controls.

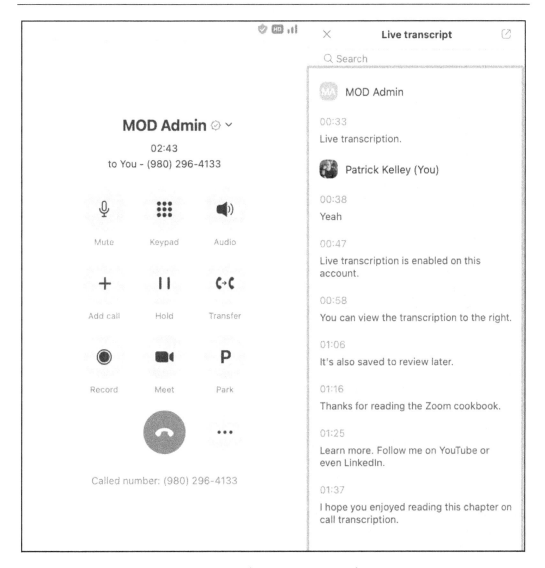

Figure 4.34 – A live transcription window

4. Should you also record the phone call, not only will live transcription be available but Zoom Phone will also record the text-to-speech conversation, enabling you to later review the transcript. You can either play the audio of the call or review just the transcript area of the recording.

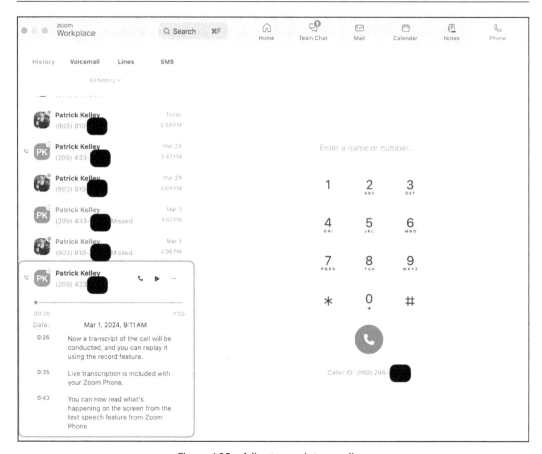

Figure 4.35 – A live transcript recording

5.   That's it. You've mastered Zoom Phone!

Using Zoom Team Chat

Zoom **Team Chat** is a robust collaboration tool designed to streamline communication and foster teamwork within organizations. With features tailored for group messaging, file sharing, and integration with other Zoom services, Zoom **Team Chat** offers a comprehensive solution for modern workplace communication needs.

One of the primary benefits of Zoom **Team Chat** is its real-time messaging capabilities. Users can create chat channels dedicated to specific projects, teams, or topics, facilitating focused discussions and ensuring that relevant information is easily accessible. Whether seeking quick feedback or sharing updates, team members can communicate efficiently without the clutter often associated with email threads.

The platform also supports file sharing, allowing users to exchange documents, images, videos, and more within the chat interface. This eliminates the need for separate file-sharing tools and promotes collaboration by providing a centralized location for all project-related assets. Additionally, Zoom **Team Chat** integrates seamlessly with cloud storage services such as Google Drive, Microsoft SharePoint, and OneDrive, further enhancing file accessibility and collaboration.

Another key feature of Zoom **Team Chat** is its integration with other Zoom services, including **Zoom Meetings** and **Zoom Phone**. Users can seamlessly transition from text-based conversations to face-to-face meetings with the click of a button, fostering deeper connections and facilitating more productive discussions. Integration with **Zoom Phone** also enables users to make voice calls directly from the chat interface, streamlining communication workflows and reducing the need for switching between different applications.

Security is a top priority for Zoom **Team Chat**, with **end-to-end encryption** (E2EE) ensuring that messages and files remain secure and confidential.

Furthermore, Zoom **Team Chat** is designed to be user-friendly, with an intuitive interface that makes it easy for team members to navigate and access the features they need. From creating channels to searching for messages and files, the platform prioritizes simplicity and efficiency, ensuring that users can focus on their work without being hindered by complex software.

In this chapter, we're going to cover the following recipes:

- Using **Team Chat**
- Creating a **Team Chat** channel
- Editing members of **Team Chat** channels
- Creating channel meetings
- Creating folders in **Team Chat**
- Setting **Team Chat** notifications
- Joining a **Team Chat** channel

Using Team Chat

Team Chat is a very powerful part of the Zoom platform. Consider it the main method for collaborating and communicating with partners, coworkers, and customers asynchronously and in real time. Understanding the structure of **Team Chat** is paramount in using this tool to its fullest potential. In this recipe, we will walk through the main sections of **Team Chat** and introduce some basic concepts. In later recipes, we will dive into exactly how to use all the features.

Getting ready

1. Navigate to the **Team Chat** icon in your Zoom client's top navigation bar:

Figure 5.1: Team Chat

There are three main areas of **Team Chat**, as highlighted in *Figure 5.2*:

- **Section 1**: This area is the left sidebar (darker area). This contains quick links to commonly used features.
- **Section 2**: This is where all chats, channels, meeting chats, and apps are located.
- **Section 3**: This area is where you actively compose chats with individuals and channels:

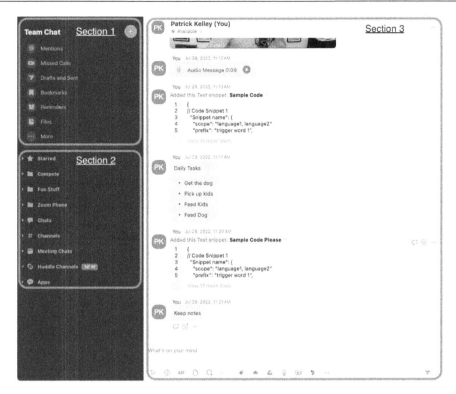

Figure 5.2: Team Chat screen

Let's dive into each of these sections in greater detail.

Section 1

This area is the left sidebar, as seen in the previous figure.

How to do it...

This contains quick links to the following areas:

- **Mentions** – When someone directly mentions you in a message with the @ symbol, such as @Patrick Kelley, you will get a notification that you have been directly referred to in a chat channel:

Figure 5.3: Mentions

- You can click **Mentions**, and a list of all the messages you were mentioned in will appear. You can jump directly to any message by clicking **Jump**:

Figure 5.4: Jump button

- You will also receive a notification in channels where you were mentioned with **@me** next to the notification. It helps alert you quickly on which channel you were mentioned, the notification to which shows on your screen as follows:

Figure 5.5: Mentions

- **Missed Calls** – Should another Zoom user attempt to contact you with audio or video and you do not answer, you will be notified there was an attempt to connect with you. Click on **Missed Calls** to see all audio calls or video calls that were missed. (**Note**: This does not apply to **Zoom Phone** or telephony calls that were missed. Those are in the **Zoom Phone History** tab you learned about in the previous chapter.)

- **Drafts and Sent** – Here, you will find chat messages that haven't been completed and sent. These are considered drafts. Also, any past chat messages that have been sent are chronologically indexed for easy reference. Finally, scheduled chat messages are listed as well. You can navigate to any area by clicking on the respective tabs:

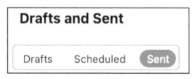

Figure 5.6: Drafts and Sent tabs

- **Bookmarks** – Should you wish to save an important chat message for easy reference, they can be labeled as bookmarks. Any message that receives this tag will be chronologically listed here. Click **...** on any message and choose **Bookmark**.

- **Reminders** – There are times when you want to set a reminder for a chat message to review later. For example, I might receive a chat message that has a task that is due. I can set a reminder on that message to review it at a later time.

To set a reminder, click on ... next to any message, then select **Remind Me**. Choose when you would like to be reminded. You can even select a custom time:

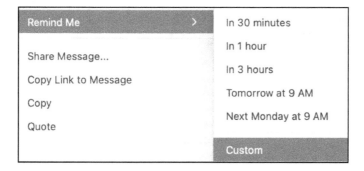

Figure 5.7: Reminders

When the reminder time has passed, you will receive a notification to alert you:

Figure 5.8: Reminder notification

- **My files** – These are all files that you have sent, that have been sent to you, or that are in chat channels you are a member of. By clicking on **Files**, you will be able to search and filter files for easy retrieval:

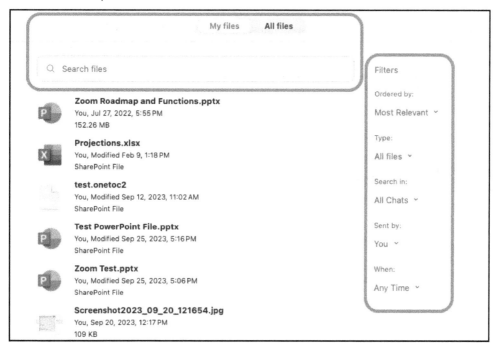

Figure 5.9: My files

- **… More** – By clicking on **…**, you will be given two additional options:

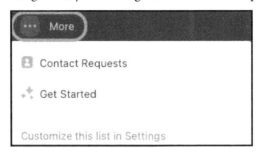

Figure 5.10: Additional options

- **Contact Requests** – Should an external user on Zoom wish to connect with you, a notification will appear here. If you accept this request, your profile information (including your status) will be visible to the contact. You can also meet and chat with this contact.

- **Get Started** – This is a self-guided tour of the basics of Zoom **Team Chat**. This is a great way to become familiar with the basic principles of **Team Chat** should this be your first time using the tool:

Customizing options.

You can completely customize the options you see in **Section 1** by clicking the **Settings** link. This will take you to your **Team Chat** settings. Check which sections you want to appear in your left sidebar:

Figure 5.11: Files

Section 2

This area is where all your team chats will be, both with individuals as well as channels:

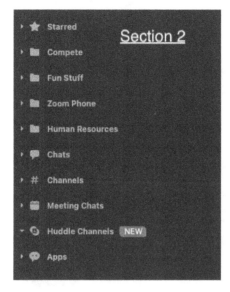

Figure 5.12: Section 2 area

How to do it...

This section contains the following options that you can utilize for your team chat:

- **Starred**: When you have users or channels that you frequently communicate with, you can *star* them. This will then place the user or channel in this section for ease of navigation. For example, I starred my boss and the important channels that I belong to:

Figure 5.13: Starred contact

Then, when I receive a chat from this individual or channel, a notification appears next to **Starred** for quick visual reference:

Figure 5.14: Starred notification

- **Folders**: Folders are a way to organize all your contacts and channels. These are custom folders you will create yourself. Notice the folder icon is before the folder name in *Figure 5.15*:

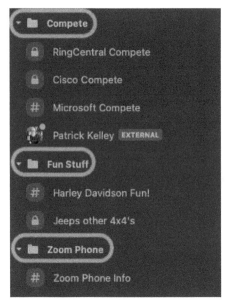

Figure 5.15: Folders

For example, you may be part of the Human Resources team and belong to many channels that are related to your job in HR such as #Benefits, #Health, or even #Payroll. You may have important people that are part of HR that you frequently communicate with. Creating a folder and placing all these channels and users in it is a great way to organize **Team Chat** (**Note**: You will learn how to create folders in a later recipe.):

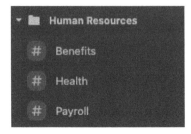

Figure 5.16: Team Chat folders

- **Chats**: This is where all chats with contacts and users will be stored. These will be listed in chronological order of recent users you have been chatting with. Both internal and external users will be listed:

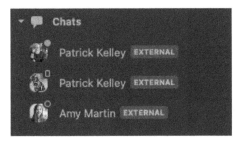

Figure 5.17: Chat users

- **Channels**: Channels allow you to create private or public groups where you can send messages, files, and images and start an instant meeting with channel members. Channels begin with a hash sign (#). These channels generally serve as longer-term collaboration forums, such as specific teams, channels serving a specific purpose or topic, and announcement channels. For example, you might wish to have a channel on a project you are working on with users inside your organization as well as external partners you may be working with. Creating a channel is a great way to collaborate with an entire team, allowing you to share chats and information quickly and easily (**Note**: We will learn how to create a channel in a later recipe.):

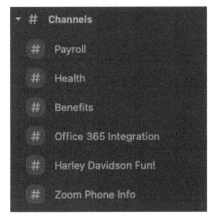

Figure 5.18: Team Chat channels

- **Meeting Chats**: Recall from a previous chapter you learned how to enable **Continuous Meeting Chats** when creating a meeting. These meeting chats are placed in this section:

Figure 5.19: Meeting Chats

Section 3

This section is where you will compose and reply to chats from individuals as well as channels:

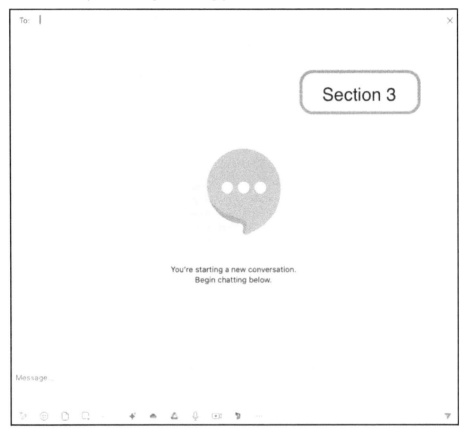

Figure 5.20: Team Chat compose

How to do it...

Section 3 contains the following discussed options:

- **To**: This is where you will type the name(s) of the individuals you wish to chat with. This can be a single person or multiple people. If you are part of an organization, all the enabled Zoom users will be in a directory. As you begin entering the person's name, Zoom will start parsing names that only contain what you entered. For example, in the following figure, I typed `Patrick`, and Zoom displayed all users and contacts that matched the typed keyword. You can also enter the email address of an external user, and they will be invited to the chat:

Figure 5.21: Team Chat compose

- **Message**: This is the area where you will enter the message you want to send to a user, group, or channel. As you begin typing the message, the **Send** icon will turn blue. When you have completed typing your chat, click the **Send** button. You will also note that there is a *rich-text* icon as well should you wish to use features beyond basic text, such as **Bold**, **Italic**, or **Underline**. Of course, no chat would be complete without fun features such as emojis and gifs:

Figure 5.22: Team Chat compose

You can also send files in **Team Chat**. Click the **File** icon and browse to the location of the file you wish to share with users or channels:

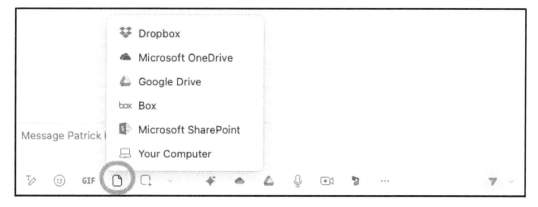

Figure 5.23: Chat files

Sometimes, it is helpful to capture a screenshot to share. This can easily be done in **Team Chat**. Click the **Screenshare** icon. Zoom allows you to capture individual program windows, or just drag your cursor over the area you wish to capture. The screenshot will appear in the message field for you to send. Also, notice that when you grab your screenshot, you can annotate it as well to highlight areas you wish to draw attention to:

Figure 5.24: Screenshot

You can also record a voice message, much like a voicemail. Just click the **Voice Message** icon. Record your dialogue, then click **Send**. Super easy. A great way to leave an audio message instead of having to type out the entire message in a chat:

Figure 5.25: Voice message

Video messaging via **Team Chat** is also a cool feature **Team Chat** provides. Click the **Video Message** icon, record a video of yourself, and send it to individuals or channels. You can even use virtual backgrounds: a great way to get your message across visually. I use this a lot to leave a more personal message for coworkers and customers. Creating a quick video message can create a more immersive feel and get your point across with your personal non-verbal expressions greater than a simple chat message:

Figure 5.26: Video message

• **Chat History**: As you compose and receive messages with individuals and channels, your dated chat history will appear. These messages are persistent, allowing you to scroll through the entire message history of your conversation:

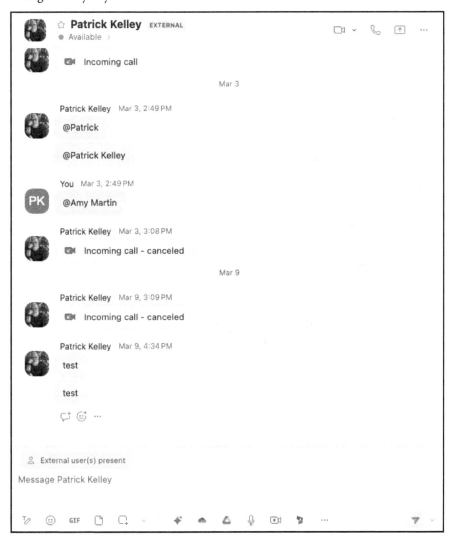

Figure 5.27: Team Chat history

You now know how to navigate Zoom **Team Chat**...

Creating a Team Chat channel

As we discussed in the previous recipe, **Team Chat** channels are a great way to create private or public groups to send messages or files. These are usually longer-term collaboration forums. Let's dive into how to create them with **Team Chat**.

How to do it...

1. Click the **Team Chat** icon at the top of your navigation bar
2. Click the + icon to the right of **Team Chat**, then choose **Channel**:

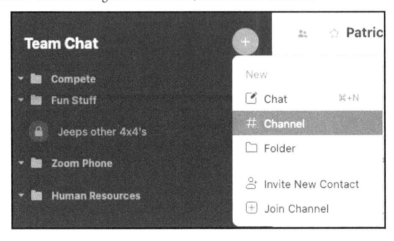

Figure 5.28: New channel

Enter the *channel name*. Choose something easily recognizable to your audience that deals with the content of the channel.

Choose your channel type. There are two options:

*   **Public** – Anyone in your organization can find, preview, and join
*   **Private** – Only users invited to the channel can join

Next, add members. This is an optional step. For a **Public** channel, users will be able to search and join the channel on their own; therefore, there may not be a need to add anyone as the channel creator. For example, you might create a channel for dog lovers in your organization. Anyone who wants to join certainly can. (**Note**: Joining a channel is the subject of the next recipe.) If you are creating a **Private** channel, you will want to add all the members of the channel that you wish to participate. For example, if you created a channel called **Employee Bonuses**, this would most likely be a channel that only a select view would need access to. Add those members here:

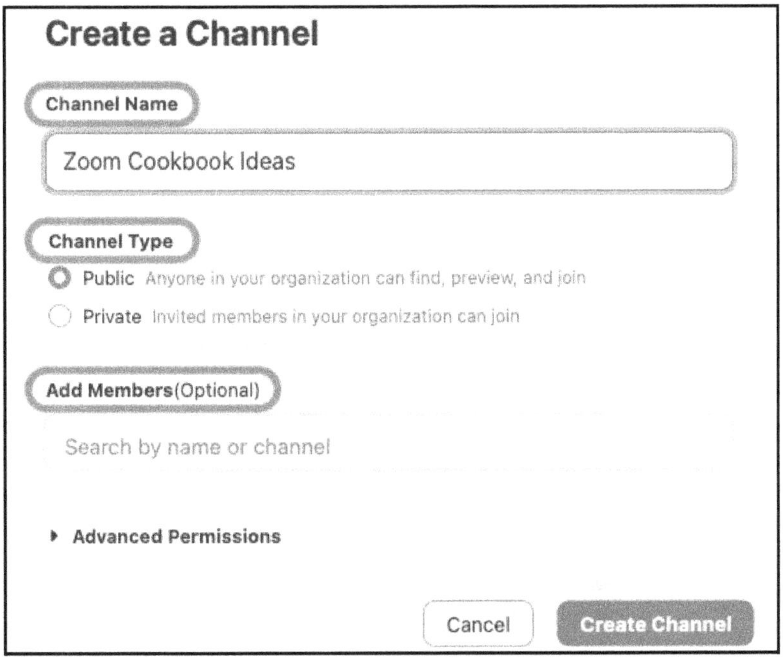

Create a Channel

Channel Name

Zoom Cookbook Ideas

Channel Type

⦿ **Public** Anyone in your organization can find, preview, and join

◯ **Private** Invited members in your organization can join

Add Members(Optional)

Search by name or channel

▸ **Advanced Permissions**

Cancel   **Create Channel**

Figure 5.29: Create a Channel

Notice the **Advanced Permissions** option. Click on it to expand this section:

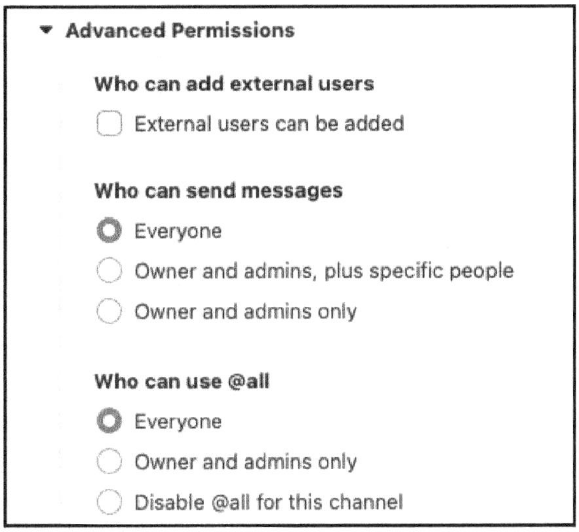

▾ **Advanced Permissions**

Who can add external users

☐ External users can be added

Who can send messages

⦿ Everyone

◯ Owner and admins, plus specific people

◯ Owner and admins only

Who can use @all

⦿ Everyone

◯ Owner and admins only

◯ Disable @all for this channel

Figure 5.30: Advanced Permissions

3. Select all the options that are needed for your channel.

4. Then, click **Create Channel**:

Figure 5.31: Create Channel

All **Public** channels with have a # icon in front of the name of the channel. All **Private** channels will have a lock icon preceding the channel name:

Figure 5.32: Creating a channel

You are now a master in **Team Chat** channels!

Editing members of Team Chat channels

Once a channel is created, you may want to add/remove members. Don't worry – this is all easily done in Zoom.

How to do it...

1. Click on any channel for which you want to add/remove members.

2. Click the figure icon:

Figure 5.33: Adding members

An **About Channel** window will appear. Click the + icon to the right of **Members**:

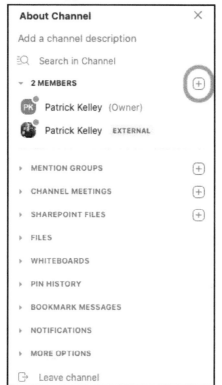

Figure 5.34: Adding members

Add any further members to the channel.

3.   To remove a member of a channel, hover over them with your mouse and click ....

4.   A new window will appear. Click **Remove**:

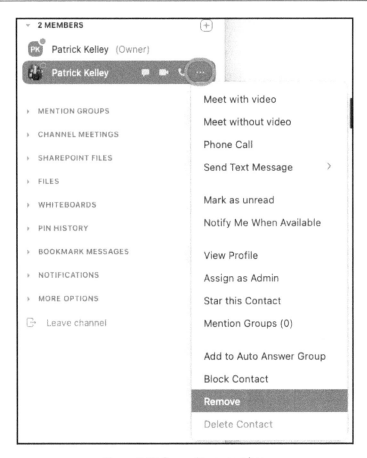

Figure 5.35: Removing a member

You are now an expert in modifying **Team Chat** members.

Creating channel meetings

You may wish to create an ad hoc meeting for all channel members to discuss an important item. Perhaps you wish to create a scheduled status meeting to review weekly updates. Creating channel meetings is a bit easier than scheduling a regular Zoom meeting and inviting everyone individually. When you create a new channel meeting, it automatically adds all the channel members, creates a continuous meeting chat, as well as creates a meeting summary. (**Note:** You will learn more about meeting summaries in *Chapter 7*)

How to do it...

1. Navigate to your **Team Chat** channel.

2. To the right, you will see a *camera* icon. Click on it to immediately start a Zoom meeting inviting all members of the channel:

Figure 5.36: Ad hoc channel meeting

Should you wish to schedule a future or recurring Zoom meeting, click the calendar icon. This will open a window for creating a scheduled Zoom meeting:

Figure 5.37: Scheduled channel meeting

Congratulations! You now know how to create channel meetings.

Creating folders in Team Chat

Folders are a great way to organize **Team Chat**. At times, we may be members of hundreds of channels, but a small fraction of those may be more important than others, and you may wish to create folders to keep similar channels in groupings for easier navigation. We discussed being a member of the Human Resources department in a previous recipe and organizing **Team Chat** channels in a folder. Let's now learn how to do that!

1. Navigate to **Team Chat** in the top navigation bar.

2. Click the + icon to the right of **Team Chat** and click **Folder**:

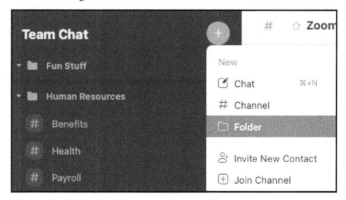

Figure 5.38: New folder

Enter your folder name. (**Note:** Folders are per user. Only you will be able to view your customized folders.)

Now, add contacts, chats, or channels to your new folder. In the following figure, I added a **Public** channel, a contact, and a **Private** channel:

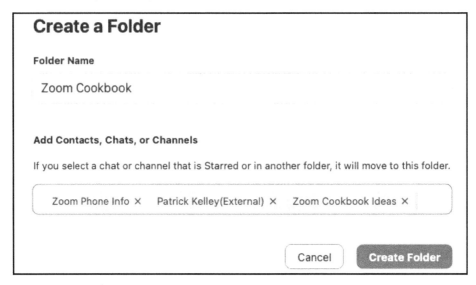

Figure 5.39: Create a Folder

3.   Once done, click the **Create Folder** button.

Should you wish to add/remove contacts, chats, or channels from your folder, simply drag and drop items into or out of your folder at any time.

You should be proud of yourself. You're an expert on **Team Chat** folders!

Setting Team Chat notifications

Being part of hundreds of channels is great for being completely informed, but a lot of times, we get inundated with thousands of messages daily. We need to control what is important and what isn't. As knowledge workers, we need to streamline which chat messages are important and what can wait for a day or two. Controlling how we are notified of incoming messages is key. Let's dive deeper into how to configure Zoom to notify us of incoming messages!

How to do it...

1. Navigate to your profile picture or icon in the top-right corner of your Zoom client and click it.

2. Then, choose **Settings** from the drop-down menu:

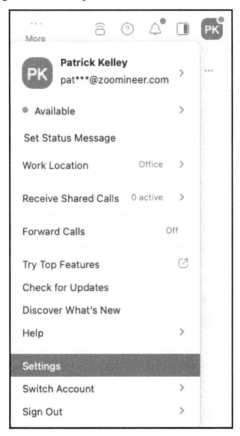

Figure 5.40: Settings menu

3. Then, choose **Team Chat** from the left navigation panel.

4. Scroll down to the **Notifications** section of your settings.

Here, you will be able to configure how you wish to be notified of all incoming chat messages from individuals as well as channels:

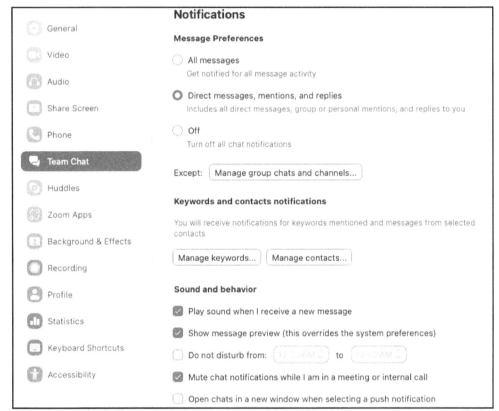

Figure 5.41: Chat notifications

Your wizard skills are now vast with chat notifications!

Joining a Team Chat channel

If you're part of an organization with multiple channels, you may wish to join them. Some channels might be targeted toward company announcements such as **Quarterly Revenue**. Other channels may be a way to engage with a community such as **Peloton Enthusiasts**. Regardless, there is a way to search and join these public channels.

How to do it...

1. Navigate to **Team Chat** in your top navigation bar.

2. Click the + icon to the right of **Team Chat**. Then, choose **Join Channel**:

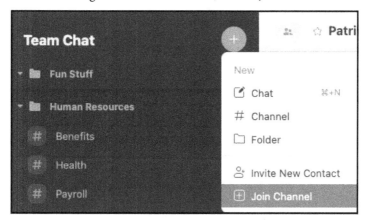

Figure 5.42: Join Channel

Enter which channel you wish to join. Search for keywords or topics.

3. Once you have discovered the channel you wish to join, click the **Join** icon.

4. The channel you just joined will now appear in the **# Channels** area in the left sidebar.

5. Congratulations – you are a **Team Chat** channel Jedi!

6
Zoom Webinars

Zoom Webinars has become an indispensable tool for businesses, educational institutions, and organizations worldwide, facilitating seamless communication and collaboration across different geographical locations. Offering a platform for hosting virtual events, presentations, workshops, and more, Zoom Webinars provides a dynamic and interactive way to engage with audiences of varying sizes.

Webinars doesn't provide meetings. It has a different function. Webinars is intended as a real-time presentation-type platform. The content is driven by hosts and panelists, not attendees. Webinars is a one-to-many type platform, meaning presenters (the host and panelist) are educating attendees about a topic. Examples of this include training, where a presentation is teaching a skill or product to hundreds if not thousands of attendees. Another example might be a company earnings call, maybe an executive roundtable, or even new feature demos. In each of these examples, hosts and/or panelists can share data, screens, and slides with thousands of attendees using Zoom Webinars.

One of the key features of Zoom Webinars is its scalability, allowing hosts to accommodate anywhere from a handful to thousands of attendees. This flexibility makes it an ideal choice for events of all magnitudes, whether it's a small team meeting or a large-scale conference. The platform's intuitive interface makes it easy for both hosts and participants to navigate, ensuring a smooth experience for everyone involved.

Zoom Webinars offers a plethora of tools and features that are designed to enhance engagement and interaction. Hosts can leverage options such as polling, reactions, Q&A, and chat functionalities to keep attendees engaged and encourage participation. These interactive elements foster a sense of community among participants, despite being physically distant, thereby enriching the overall webinar experience.

Zoom Webinars also includes registration as a feature., allowing the webinar hosts to collect names, email addresses, and other information from the registrants. This also acts as a security barrier as registrants are required to confirm before entering the webinar. Also, as a webinar host, you can control who is allowed to enter the webinar.

Furthermore, Zoom Webinars provides robust analytics and reporting capabilities, enabling hosts to gain valuable insights into attendee behavior, engagement levels, and other pertinent metrics. This data can inform future webinar strategies, allowing hosts to refine their content and delivery for optimal results.

In this chapter, we are going to cover the following recipes:

- Creating a Zoom webinar

- Creating a webinar template

- Setting up registration

- Implementing polls/quizzes

- Implementing surveys

- Implementing Q&A

- Implementing chat

- Learning webinar controls

- Using recordings

- Using reports

Technical requirements

Zoom Webinars is a license-based product from Zoom, so a Zoom Webinars license is required to create webinars (note that no license is required for attendees). The license cost is based on the number of attendees. Zoom offers many different webinar licenses, starting at 500 attendees, but they can go to 10,000+. To read more about the pricing, visit Zoom Webinar Pricing: `https://zoom.us/pricing/events`.

Creating Zoom Webinars

Webinars are scheduled as future events; therefore, they need to be created before the webinar date. They are created in your Zoom portal and not from the Zoom client.

How to do it...

Follow these steps:

1. Sign into your `Zoom portal` and navigate to **Webinars** from the left navigation tab:

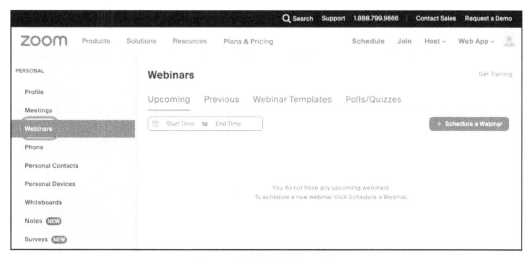

Figure 6.1: The Webinars tab

2.   Then, select + **Schedule a Webinar**:

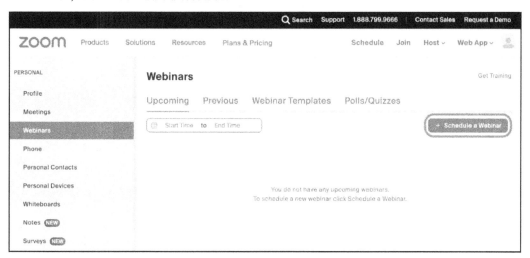

Figure 6.2: + Schedule a Webinar

3.   A **Schedule a Webinar** window will appear.

4.   Enter all the appropriate information for your webinar, such as topic, date/time, length, and so on. Most of these are self-explanatory. We will dive deeper into advanced webinar options in the *Learning webinar controls* recipe.

5. Once you've entered all this information and chosen all pertinent options, scroll to the bottom of **Create webinar** and click **Schedule**. (Note that after you click **Schedule**, a window will appear with additional settings. We will cover these in additional recipes, such as *Implementing Q&A*, *Implementing chat*, and *Implementing polls/quizzes*, but for now, this recipe will guide you through how to create a simple webinar). This can be seen in the following screenshot:

Figure 6.3: Schedule

6. Once you've created and scheduled your webinar, Zoom will create a unique URL for it. You can use this URL to advertise your webinar on LinkedIn or perhaps your personal or business web page. You can also share this link via an email campaign to promote attendance to your webinar.

7. If you need to edit or delete any scheduled webinar, click the **Webinars** tab on the left navigation page. Then, hover over the respective webinar, and click **Edit** or **Delete**:

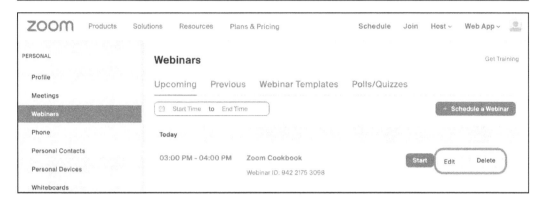

Figure 6.4: Edit/delete a webinar

8. Once you are ready to start the scheduled webinar, hover over it with your mouse cursor and click **Start**:

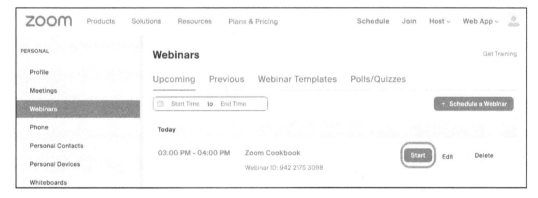

Figure 6.5: Start

9. That's it! You've mastered how to schedule a Zoom webinar.

Creating a webinar template

When you schedule a webinar, there may be times you will want to use the same settings on other webinars. For example, you might have a webinar on new product launches that you do every month. Instead of setting up a new webinar every time and manually picking the settings, you can just use a template with all your previous settings already saved. You can save these settings as a template so that when you go to schedule a similar webinar, you can quickly and easily use the same options with a configured template.

How to do it...

Follow these steps:

1. Schedule a new webinar, as you did in the previous recipe.

2. Once you've configured and entered all the information for your webinar, click **Schedule**. A review window will appear, outlining all the options you selected for your webinar. Click **Save as Template**:

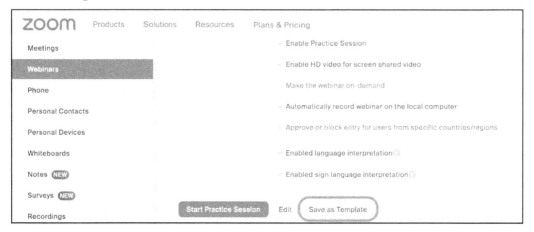

Figure 6.6: Save as Template

3. A new window will open to **Save as a Webinar Template**. Enter the name of your template and then click **Save as Template**:

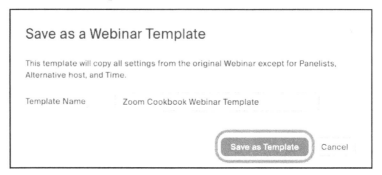

Figure 6.7: Naming and saving the template

4. The next time you schedule a new webinar, your template will appear in the **Template** drop-down menu:

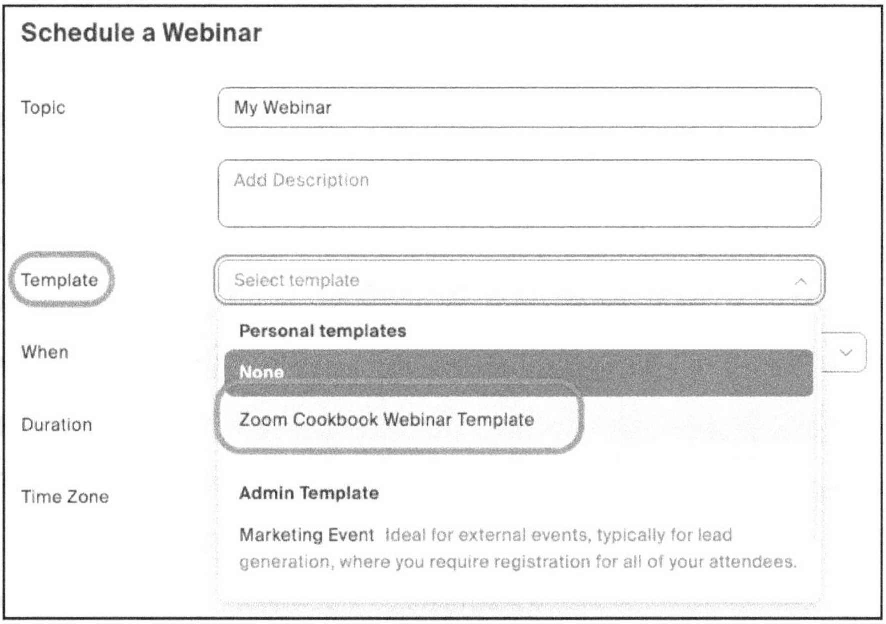

Figure 6.8: Zoom Cookbook Webinar Template

> **Note**
>
> This recipe is for personal templates and can be used only by you as a user. If your Zoom admin has set up additional *Admin Templates*, those can also be used instead. Admin templates can be used by everyone in your organization.

5. You've now mastered creating webinar templates!

Setting up registration

Zoom Webinars can be set up to include attendee registration. The host or organizer of the webinar can create a registration page for all users who wish to attend the webinar. Attendees of the webinar will provide contact information such as name and email address, which will inform the organizer of those wishing to attend. The registration process helps organizers manage attendance, send reminders and updates to participants, and gather necessary information for follow-up purposes. An example of when you might want to include registration is during a webinar where you might be trying to sell goods or services. As the webinar organizer, you will have information about everyone who registered to attend, such as their name, email address, and phone number. You can then use this information to follow up with registered users, increasing your sales and networking ability.

How to do it...

Follow these steps:

1. Create a new webinar, as you learned in the previous recipe.

2. Scroll down in your webinar options until you see **Registration**. Toggle it on:

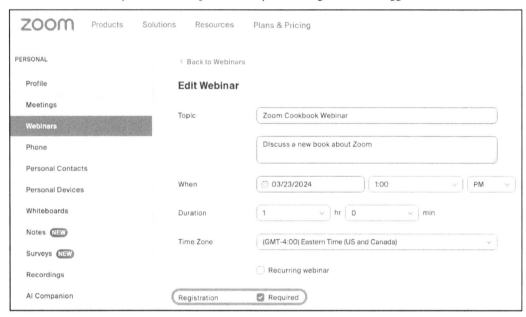

Figure 6.9: Registration

3. Once you've finished scheduling your webinar, you will have a **Registration Link** value that can be sent and advertised for your attendees.

4. As you may recall from the *Creating Zoom Webinars* recipe, when creating a webinar, when you click **Schedule**, a review window appears. This is where your **Registration Link** is located, as shown here:

Figure 6.10: Registration Link

5. You can now copy this link and advertise your webinar to your potential attendees. For example, you can email this link to a prospective list of users who might be interested in your webinar. You can advertise your webinar on social media pages such as LinkedIn, YouTube, or Instagram.

6. Once your potential attendees click on the registration link, they will be taken to your Zoom Webinars registration page, where they can enter their information, as shown here:

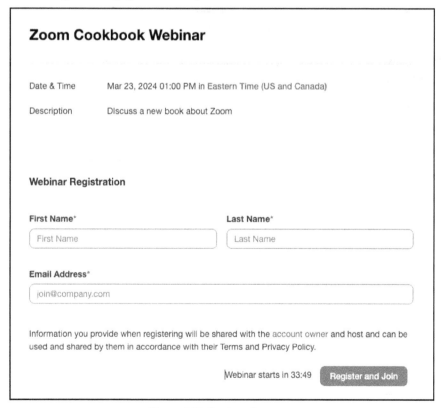

Figure 6.11: Registration page

7. Once registered, the attendee will receive an acknowledgment screen that they have successfully registered. They will also receive an email with a calendar invite for the registered webinar.

8. By default, your webinar will be set to **Automatically Approve**. Anyone who registers with their name and email address will be automatically approved to attend the webinar. You can change this to **Manual Approval** for stricter control of who is allowed to view your webinar.

9. To change the approval process, go to the webinar that you created in the Zoom portal. Then, hover over your webinar and click on the **My Webinar** link:

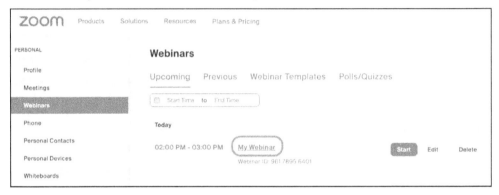

Figure 6.12: My Webinar

10. A **Manage Webinar** screen will appear. Scroll to the bottom of the page. Click the **Invitations** tab. Now, navigate to the **Registrations Setting** area and click **Edit**:

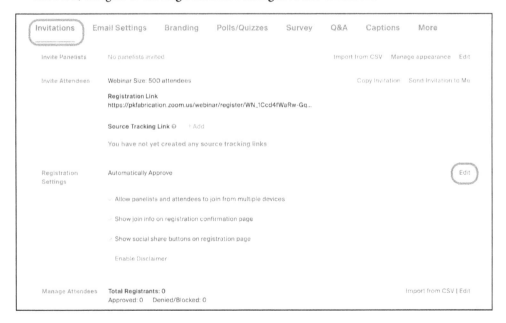

Figure 6.13: Registration approval

11. A new **Registration** window will open. Select **Manually Approve** and then click **Save All**.

12. Also, note the **Other options** section. Several of the options are checked by default. Should you wish to toggle these on/off, you can, but for most webinars, these should be left alone unless you have a specific need to turn them off:

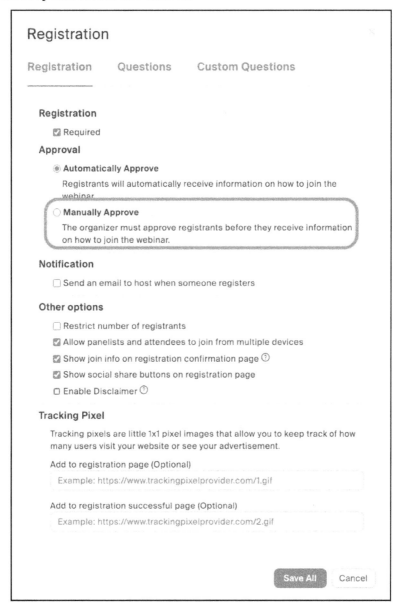

Figure 6.14: Manually Approve

13. Notice that there are additional questions you can ask during registration by clicking the **Questions** tab. By default, **First Name** and **email** are required questions, and **Last Name** is set to required but can be set to not required. Choose all the questions you want to include in your attendee registration and whether they are required or optional. There is a **Custom Questions** option next to the **Questions** tab where you can enter additional questions:

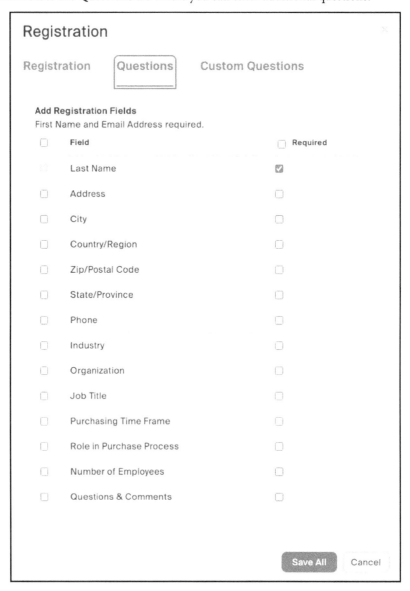

Figure 6.15: Additional questions

14. Once a user answers all the questions from the registration page when it's set to **Manually Approved**, they will see a notice that their registration is awaiting approval:

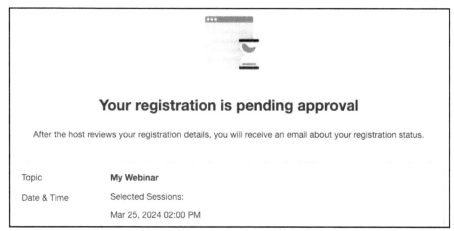

Figure 6.16: Pending approval

15. As the webinar organizer, you will need to approve all pending registered users. To do that, click on your webinar link, like you did in *Step 8*. Again, scroll to the bottom and make sure you are on the **Invitations** tab. Under **Manage Attendees**, click **Edit**:

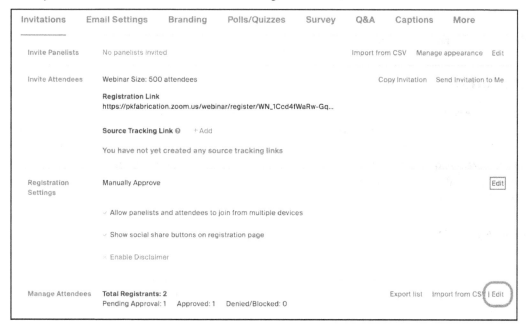

Figure 6.17: Manually Approve

16. All users that have registered and are awaiting approval will be located in the **Pending Approval** tab. You can approve or deny each registrant by checking the box next to their name and clicking **Approve** or **Deny**:

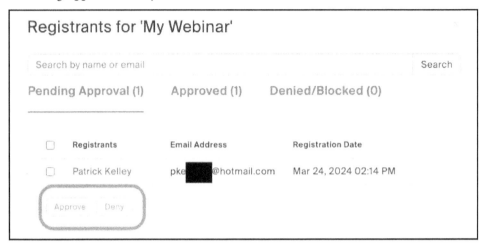

Figure 6.18: Pending Approval

17. The approved user will then receive an email with a calendar invitation and a unique join link to the webinar.

That's it. You've now mastered Zoom webinar registration!

Implementing Polls/Quizzes

Webinars are certainly a great way to present information with audio, video, and presentations. But to truly harness the power of webinars, you need to engage your audience or even have them engage with each other Zoom Webinars has many features that allow for greater immersion into your webinar. Polls/Quizzes are questions you can ask your audience *during* the webinar. You can use polls to gauge interest or mood in a topic or perhaps quizzes for your audience to determine their knowledge of the material you just presented.

How to do it...

Follow these steps:

1. Click on a previously created webinar link or create a new webinar and scroll down to the bottom of your webinar options screen:

Figure 6.19: My Webinar

2. Click on the **Polls/Quizzes** tab. To create a new Poll/Quiz, click the + **Create** button:

Figure 6.20: Polls/Quizzes

3. By default, a **Poll** window appears. To create a quiz, toggle the **Make it a quiz** option. Polls are questions you ask the attendees about their opinions on a certain topic. For example, "What is your favorite color?" There isn't a right/wrong answer. A quiz is a specific question with a definite right/wrong answer – for example, "What color is an orange?" Use both during your webinar to elicit engagement from your audience. Enter all the information for your poll or quiz:

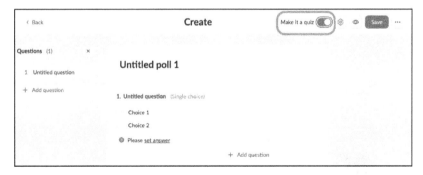

Figure 6.21: Quiz toggle

You can change what kind of poll or quiz you are creating by clicking to the right of your question. Here, you have many ways to design how your attendees answer:

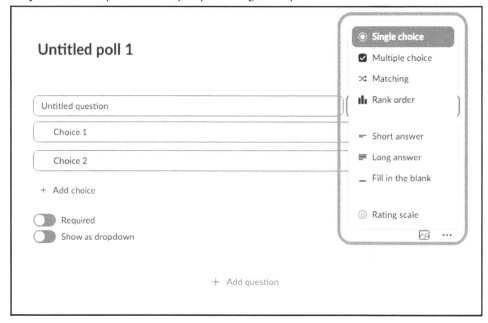

Figure 6.22: Question choices

4. You can also choose to set answers to be anonymous from the *Settings* icon if you want. By default, all answers are not anonymous. For example, you might ask a question about the salary range of the participants; they probably wouldn't answer if it weren't anonymous:

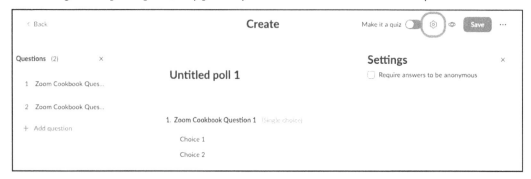

Figure 6.23: Settings

5. You can preview what your questions will look like to your attendees by clicking the *Preview* icon. Once you're done entering all poll/quiz information, click **Save**. You can save questions to your library so that you can use them again for other webinars:

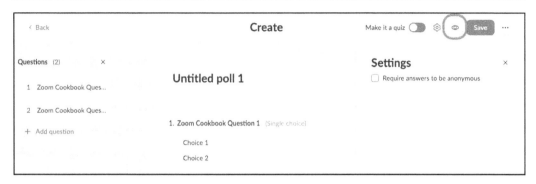

Figure 6.24: Preview

6. Once you start your webinar, all your pre-created **Polls/Quizzes** can be launched whenever you want by clicking the **Polls/Quizzes** button in your **Meetings Control** menu. You learned about this in *Chapter 1*:

Figure 6.25: The Polls/Quizzes button

7. Once you click the **Polls/Quizzes** button, all your pre-created questions will appear in a new window. Hover over the question you want to ask your attendees and click **Launch**:

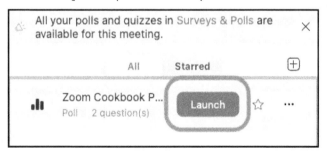

Figure 6.26: Launch

8. Your webinar attendees will see the questions you launched and will be able to answer them and submit their results.

9. As a best practice, don't create overly complicated questions. These should be easy to read and answer within seconds. You don't want your audience waiting around for too long for everyone to answer. When you're done with a poll or quiz, click the **End Poll** button:

Figure 6.27: End Poll

10. As the webinar host, you can **Share Results** of the poll/quiz with webinar attendees to view. Use the **Share Results** and **Stop Sharing** buttons to begin and stop sharing when you are done:

Figure 6.28: Share Results

11. You can find additional options by clicking **...** next to the **Share Results** button:

Figure 6.29: Additional options

12. So far, we've covered pre-created polls/quizzes. Zoom also allows you to create real-time **Polls/Quizzes** during the webinar. For example, let's say a new topic came up during a panelist discussion and you want to poll the audience's reaction. Simply click on the + button and follow the steps for creating your questions:

Figure 6.30: Additional questions

13. That's it – you've mastered how to use **Polls/Quizzes**.

Implementing surveys

Surveys are questions that you can ask *after* a webinar in a survey, right after the webinar is over, or perhaps send out an email survey post-webinar. Maybe you would like to get a survey of how the audience liked the webinar or even ask what future topics they would like to hear about. Using Surveys is a great way to get attendee feedback.

How to do it...

Follow these steps:

1. Create or edit a webinar in the Zoom portal. Scroll to the bottom of your webinar creation/edit page, as you learned in the previous recipe. Click the **Survey** tab, click +**Add Survey**, and then choose **Create Survey**. (Note that you can also use a third-party survey such as Google Forms or Survey Monkey for this). This can be seen in the following screenshot:

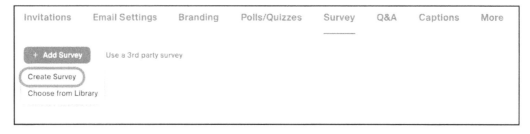

Figure 6.31: Survey options

2. A new window will appear, much like when you created **Polls/Quizzes**. As this is a survey, only questions can be entered, not polls. Add as many survey questions as you wish. As a best practice, make survey questions short and easy to answer to increase participation in your survey.

3. Just like **Polls/Quizzes**, there are additional options you can use for your questions. For example, you can also change background colors or preview your survey questions. Choose which options you would like and click **Save**:

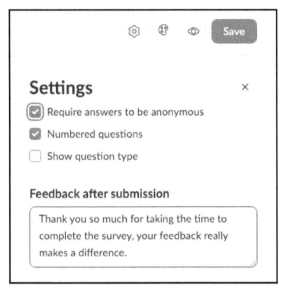

Figure 6.32: Additional options

4. By default, the survey will appear to all webinar attendees in a browser. You also have the option to include a follow-up email if you wish. To change survey options, click **Edit** next to **Survey Options**:

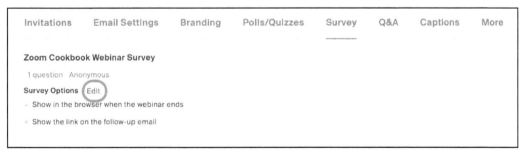

Figure 6.33: Survey Options

5. The **Edit Survey Settings** window will appear. Toggle which options you want and click **Save**:

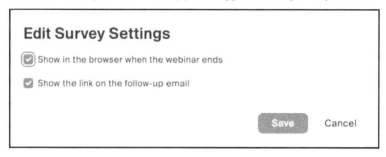

Figure 6.34: Edit Survey Settings

6. As host, make sure you remind your audience to fill out the survey at the end of the webinar!

7. When you end your webinar, a browser will appear with your survey questions, and/or an email will be sent to all webinar attendees, depending on which options you selected.

8. Once your survey has been sent out via browser or email, you should give it some time before you view the results. For example, if you chose the browser-only option, you will likely get your results within an hour as it is easy for the attendees to choose whether they want to answer the survey or not. If you used the email option, those results will take longer to gather as people typically engage with email at a slower pace than a browser window immediately after a webinar.

9. To review the survey results, navigate to the **Survey** tab in the Zoom portal and click on the webinar survey you wish to review:

Figure 6.35: Surveys

That's it – you've mastered Surveys.

Implementing Q&A

This feature lets the audience ask questions during the webinar. Allowing attendees to ask questions can elicit great feedback on how the webinar is going and allows a more immersive and personal feel to the webinar. Questions can be answered in real time during the webinar for attendees to view. These are answered by the host(s) or panelist(s) of the webinar. This can be done live, though answers can be typed in response.

How to do it...

Follow these steps:

1. Create or edit a webinar, go to the **Options** area, and check **Q&A**:

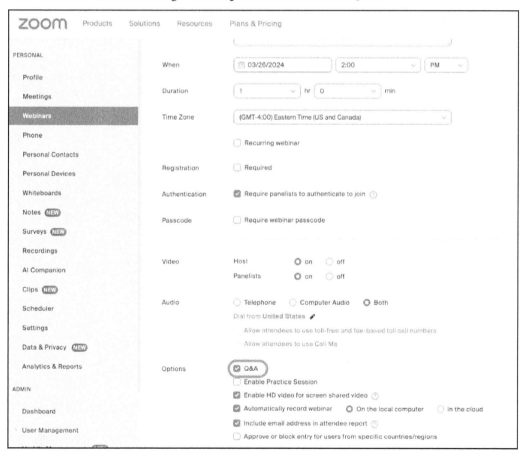

Figure 6.36: Enabling Q&A

2. To view your Q&A options, scroll to the bottom of your webinar creation window. Then, click on the **Q&A** tab. Note that the default options are prefixed with green checks. If you wish to change the default, click the **Edit** link:

Figure 6.37: The Q&A tab

3. You can now configure your Q&A to what fits your webinar needs best, then click **Save**. As shown in *Figure 6.38*, I've allowed attendees to upvote and comment. This increases audience engagement and sentiment:

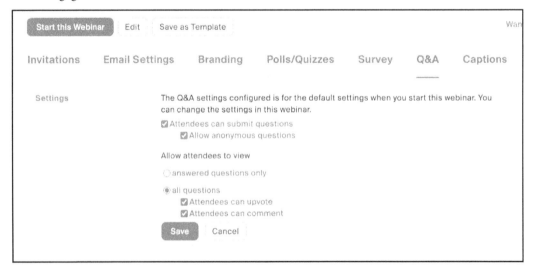

Figure 6.38: Q&A options

4. Once you start your webinar, attendees will now have a **Q&A** icon in their **Meetings Control** bar:

Figure 6.39: Q&A icon

5. Once a webinar attendee clicks the **Q&A** icon, they will now have the option to submit questions to the hosts and panelists. If configured, users will also be able to send questions anonymously:

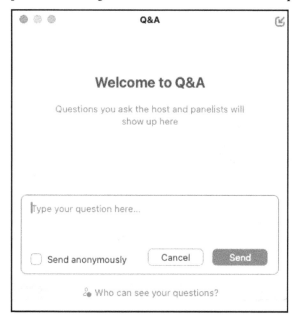

Figure 6.40: The Q&A window

6. As the webinar host, you will have a Q&A window that will give attendees control over the questions. You will see all submitted questions. You can choose to **Answer live** right from the webinar, or you can choose to **Type answer**. The best practice for a webinar is to have a co-host or panelist in charge of answering questions. Sometimes, as a webinar presenter, it is difficult to multitask when it comes to presenting content as well as answering questions:

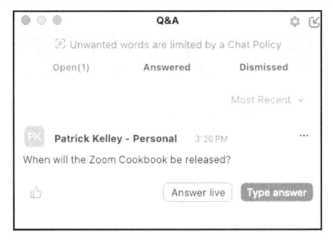

Figure 6.41: The Q&A control window

7. If you choose to **Answer live**, the question will now be tagged with **You would like to answer this question live**. Once you're done answering the questions, click **Done**. This will move the question to the **Answered** tab:

Figure 6.42: Answer live

8. If you prefer to type an answer, you can choose to send the answer back privately to the submitter. Alternatively, you can answer the question and then click **Send**, at which point the question will be posted for all attendees to view:

Figure 6.43: Typing an answer

9. As a host or panelist, you can also choose to **Dismiss** or **Delete** the question entirely if it's inappropriate or not related to the webinar and you don't wish the attendees to see it:

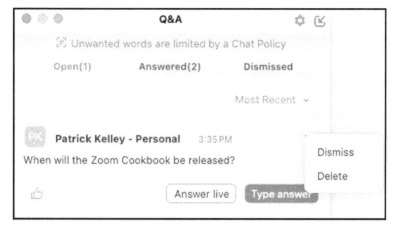

Figure 6.44: Dismiss or Delete

10. Webinar attendees will also be able to comment on the question as well as upvote the questions if this has been configured during webinar creation. All attendees will be able to view these items:

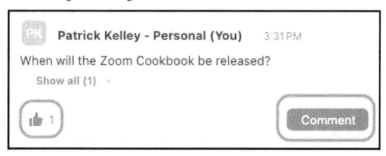

Figure 6.45: Comment and upvote

That's it! You've mastered how to use Q&A during a webinar.

Implementing chat

As we learned in *Chapter 5*, Zoom Team Chat is a great way to communicate and collaborate. We can also implement in-webinar chat capabilities. This allows attendees, hosts, and panelists to chat during the webinar either as a group or privately if configured. Chat allows users to comment on items being presented during the webinar. For example, during a webinar, you might introduce a thought-provoking topic that users want to discuss. They can use chat during the webinar to continue the discussion or comment on past ones. You can also disable chat if you don't want participants to be able to communicate with each other or perhaps you only want them to use Q&A for discussion. For very large or public webinars, it might be a good idea to disable chat to keep attendees focused on the webinar presentation.

How to do it...

1. First, you must enable **Webinar chat** at the account level. To do so, log into the Zoom portal and navigate to **Settings** from the left navigation window.

2. Click the **Meetings** tab, then choose **In Meeting (Basic)**:

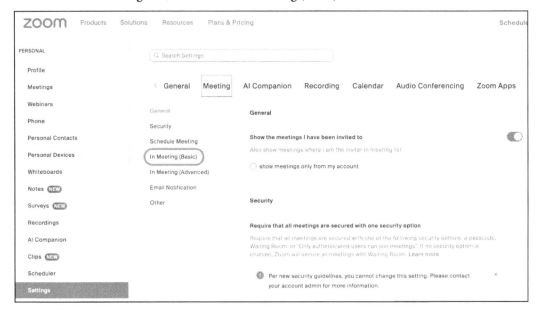

Figure 6.46: Zoom portal

3. Scroll down until you see **Webinar chat**. Verify that **Webinar chat** is set to **Enabled**:

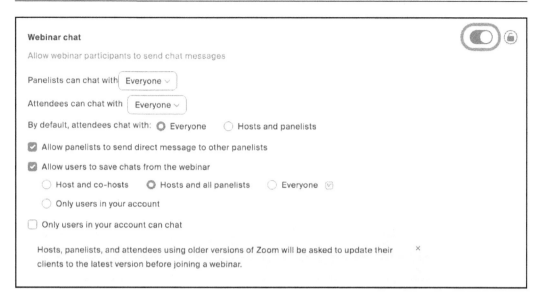

Figure 6.47: Webinar chat

4. Configure who can participate and click **Save**. In this example, I allowed **Everyone** to be able to participate in the chat, but only **Hosts and panelists** can save chats. Choose the options that meet your needs.

5. Now, any new webinar you create will have the chat settings from *Step 3* applied. A **Chat** icon will appear in the **Meetings Control** bar during a webinar for all attendees:

Figure 6.48: Chat icon

6. Participants will now be able to click the **Chat** icon and chat among hosts and panelists. This is similar to what you learned about in the *Continuous Meeting Chat* recipe.

7. Attendees can also direct chats to individual users, **Host and Panelists**, and **Everyone**, depending on your configuration from *Step 2*, by clicking on the **To:** drop-down menu:

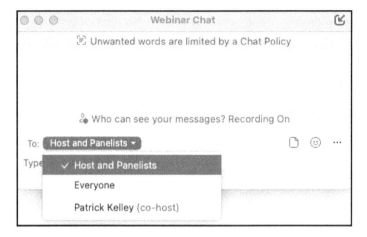

Figure 6.49: Webinar Chat

That's it – you've mastered chat!

Learning webinar controls

Just like Zoom meetings, Zoom Webinars has the exact look and feel for controlling your audio, video, and screen sharing. Recall that webinars have hosts and panelists, who are the presenters of content, and attendees, who are viewers; therefore, the controls that a user sees will look different. Let's dive into how a webinar is controlled.

How to do it...

Follow these steps:

1. Start any scheduled webinar.

2. The **Meeting Control** bar will appear at the bottom of your webinar, just as it does in **Meetings**. You should be completely familiar with all these controls as a host or panelist. These controls work exactly like they do in Zoom meetings and you can control your audio, video, screen share, whiteboard, and more. In the previous recipes, we reviewed **Chat**, **Q&A**, and **Polls/Quizzes**:

Figure 6.50: The Meeting Control bar (hosts and panelists)

3. Attendees of the webinar have a more limited **Meeting Control** bar since, as an attendee, you are viewing and consuming the presentation and not collaborating with the hosts and panelists. Notice that attendees can't share video or audio or share content:

Figure 6.51: The Meeting Control bar (attendees)

4. Now that you understand webinar controls, let's take a look at participant controls. From the host's **Meeting Control** bar, click the **Participants** icon. A separate window will open to the right of your webinar. This window contains all your panelists and attendees:

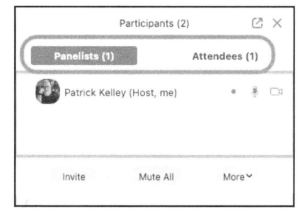

Figure 6.52: Panelists/Attendees

5. In the following screenshot, you'll notice I have one panelist, but if you have multiple hosts/panelists, they will all be listed here. Hover over any panelists you want to control; notice you have options that appear to the right of the user:

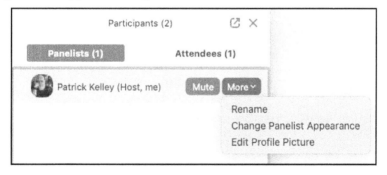

Figure 6.53: Panelist controls

You will be able to control items such as the panelist's name and profile pictures.

Now, click on the **Attendees** tab to learn how to control participants in your webinar.

6.   Hover over the attendee you wish to control. You will see several options appear to the right of the user:

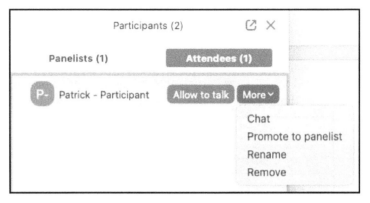

Figure 6.54: Attendee controls

7.   Now, you can interact with the attendee with your additional options.

For example, you can allow the attendee to share audio with the **Allow to talk** option. When clicked, the attendee will receive a prompt to **Unmute** so that they can be heard. A use case when you would use this feature is when an attendee has a good question in Q&A and you want everyone in the webinar to hear the question. You can allow the attendee to talk and they can ask the question live:

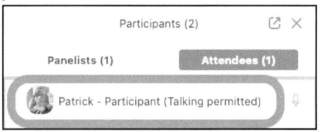

Figure 6.55: Talking permitted (attendees)

8.   You can take this one step further and promote an attendee to a full panelist:

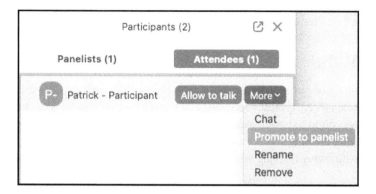

Figure 6.56: Promote to panelist

Once promoted, the user will have to agree to be a panelist from their client. This will move the user from **Attendee** into the **Panelists** area.

9. Now, hover over your new panelist; notice that you have even more options to control:

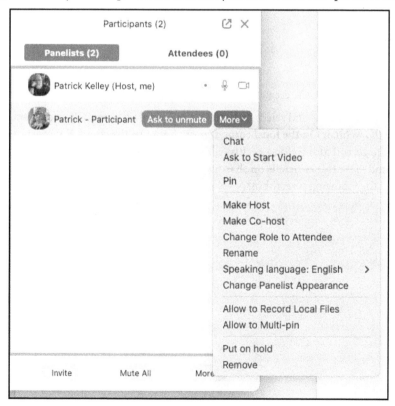

Figure 6.57: Panelists controls

That's it – you've mastered webinar controls.

Using recordings

Recordings can be set up when creating a webinar, but they can also be started from the Zoom client during a webinar. Webinars are typically recorded and then made available for users who were unable to attend. This allows you to use your webinars multiple times to reach a greater audience. A great deal of work can go into creating and presenting content for a webinar. A lot of times, you don't want that to be just a one-time event, giving your webinar a longer shelf life for consumption for a bigger audience to view.

Recording a webinar

You will most likely want to record all your webinars. This will give you the ability to share them later with an audience that wasn't unable to attend the live webinar. You can also edit the video and audio after your webinar should you want to share smaller videos on social media, such as YouTube, Instagram, or maybe even your website.

How to do it...

Follow these steps:

1. From the Zoom portal, create a new webinar or edit an existing one.

2. Scroll down to **Options** and select **Automatically record webinar**. Choose whether you wish to record the webinar **On the local computer** or choose **In the cloud**. For most use cases, you will want to record to the cloud as this will create a shareable URL for your users to quickly click on and view. (More details on sharing will be covered in the following recipe). This can be seen in the following screenshot:

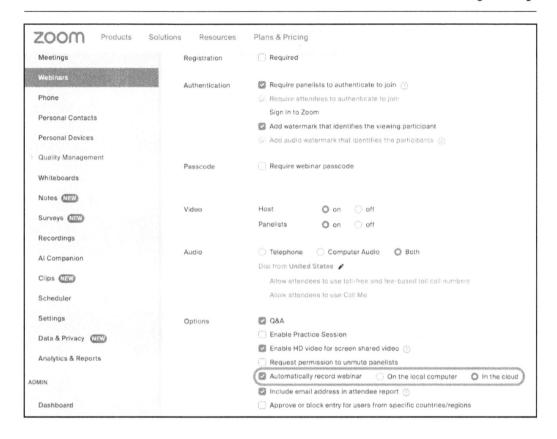

Figure 6.58: Recording from the portal

3. When you start your webinar, it will start recording automatically and stop recording when you end the webinar.

4. An alternate method to start recording is from the Zoom client during your webinar. From your **Meetings Control** bar, click the **Record** icon. You will be given the choice to record locally or record to the cloud. Just as in meetings, you can pause and start the recording as you wish from the **Record** icon:

Figure 6.59: Recording from the client

> **Note**
>
> Attendees of your webinar will be notified visually that the webinar is being recorded as well as verbally when they join as they'll see a message stating **Recording in progress**.

Sharing recordings

The whole point of recording webinars is to share them with attendees who might not have been able to attend the live webinar. You can even share your webinar on social media platforms or even on your website as a video-on-demand feature for your prospective customers to click and view.

How to do it...

Follow these steps:

1. Once you have ended the webinar, the recording will be available to share from the Zoom portal. Note that if you recorded locally, the recording file will be saved to your PC/Mac. This location can be found/changed by going to the **Settings** area of your Zoom client, clicking the **Recording** tab, and then going to **Store my recordings at:**:

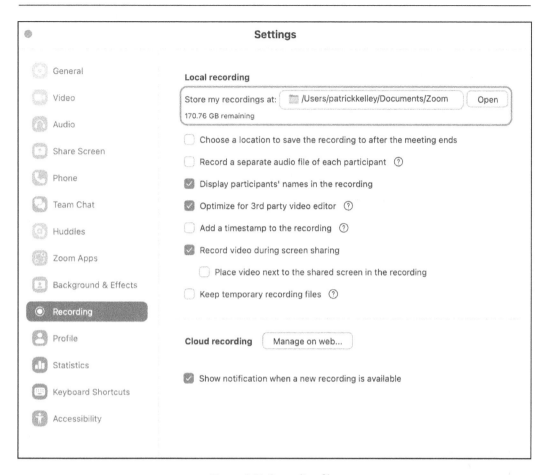

Figure 6.60: Recording files

2.   From the Zoom portal, click the **Recordings** tab. All your available **Zoom Meeting** and **Zoom Webinar** recordings will be here. Both cloud as well as local recordings will be listed here:

Figure 6.61: Recording list

3. Check the webinar recording you wish to share from the list, then click **Share**. Another window will open:

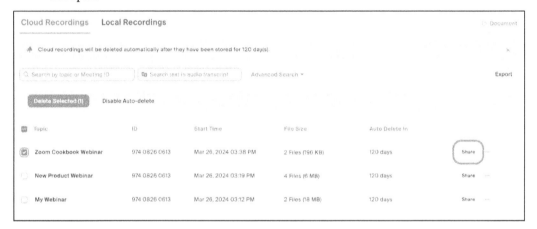

Figure 6.62: Sharing a webinar

You can now copy the **Shareable Link** and **Passcode** details for distribution. You can share this link with whomever you wish to view the webinar. This link can be shared via email, chat, web pages, or social media for ease of distribution and viewership:

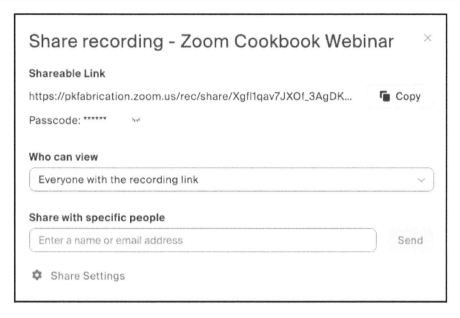

Figure 6.63: The Share recording screen

4. You can also change the permissions of who is allowed to view the webinar. Notice the **Who can view** option. If you click on this area, other options become available. Pick the one that is most appropriate for your sharing needs. By default, the **Everyone with the recording** link will be chosen:

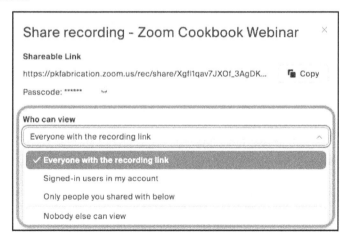

Figure 6.64: Who can view

5. You can **Share** your webinar with specific people or email addresses from this screen, or you can always send the link via Team Chat or email later:

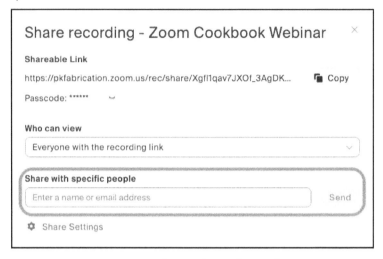

Figure 6.65: Share with specific people

6. Click the **Share Settings** link for additional sharing options:

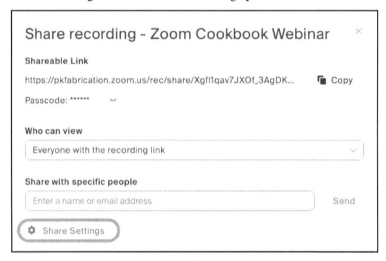

Figure 6.66: Share Settings

7. You can adjust the permissions and options of what viewers can do with your webinar recording from this screen. There are many use cases where you could toggle each of these on or off. For example, you might not want attendees to download your webinar and share it with others. Take some time to consider what is appropriate for your particular webinar before clicking **Save**:

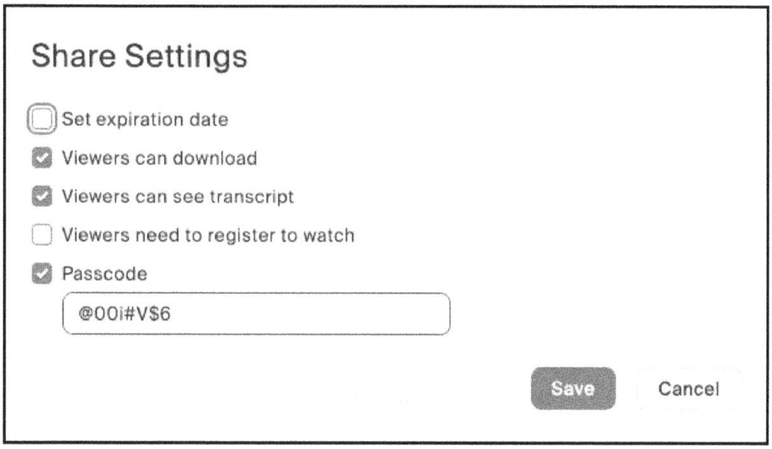

Share Settings

☐ Set expiration date

☑ Viewers can download

☑ Viewers can see transcript

☐ Viewers need to register to watch

☑ Passcode

    @00i#V$6

[Save]   Cancel

Figure 6.67: Share Settings

8. You've now become a Zoom webinar recording expert!

Using reports

In this final recipe, we will cover analytics and reports. Webinar reports allow admins and hosts to generate different metrics and information reports. These reports will allow hosts and organizers of webinars to understand registration and attendee numbers and review Q&A, polls, as well as survey results. For example, after the webinar, the host would want to review all the attendees' names and email addresses for individual follow-up for potential sales opportunities. Perhaps the hosts would like to review the Q&A during the webinar to see what questions attendees asked during the webinar. Also, reviewing the survey results of the webinar is vital to understanding how your message landed and if the attendees liked the webinar. This could be vital in understanding how your webinar presentation was received by your attendees.

How to do it...

Follow these steps:

1. Sign into the Zoom portal.

2. Navigate to the **Analytics & Reports** tab, choose **Usage Reports**, and click **Webinar**:

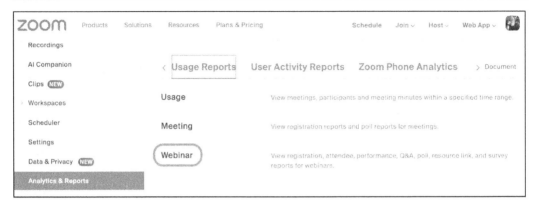

Figure 6.68: Webinar reports

3. Under **Step 1: Select Report Type** (*Figure 6.69*), select which report you wish to generate. Once you've selected your report, a search screen will open (**Step 2: Choose a Webinar** (*Figure 6.69*)). (Note that if you have questions about what a report includes, click the question mark icon to the right of the report; a description of the fields will open below the reports. Only one report can be selected at a time.)

4. Choose which webinar you will generate reports from. Use the date search fields or Webinar ID to find your specific webinar.

5. Next, select which option you want to generate in the report and click the **Generate CSV Report** button:

Figure 6.69: Generate CSV Report

6. Your report will now be generated and downloaded to your browser's `Downloads` folder as a CSV file. You can open this file with an application such as Microsoft Excel to review the data.

7. You've done it! You're a webinar report master!

7
AI Companion

Zoom AI Companion is a powerful addition that streamlines communication, enhances productivity, and makes your Zoom experience even more efficient. It is included at no extra cost to paid Zoom users. AI Companion is woven into many of the Zoom features and is continually expanding to make users more productive and efficient.

In this chapter, we're going to cover the following main topics:

- Enabling AI Companion
- Using AI Companion in meetings
- Using AI Companion in email
- Using AI Companion in Team Chat
- Using AI Companion in Zoom Phone
- Using AI Companion in Whiteboard

Enabling AI Companion

By default, AI Companion features are disabled. You must manually enable each AI Companion feature for users in the account. This is done for security and privacy reasons as Zoom uses information such as meetings to train the **large language model** (**LLM**) of your Zoom account. Zoom doesn't use customer information to train their model, so you will have to enable AI Companion in your account and use your own information to train AI Companion. The more you use it, the smarter it gets.

How to do it...

Follow these steps:

1. Sign in to your Zoom portal with administrator rights.
2. Choose **Settings** and then click **AI Companion**:

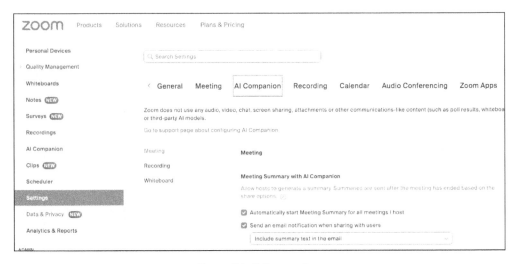

Figure 7.1: AI Companion

These settings will only apply to you, not your entire account. In later recipes, we will apply AI Companion features that are enabled at an account level.

3. Toggle which AI Companion features you want to be turned on just for your user. We will dive deeper into each of these features in subsequent recipes, but for now, you must know how to turn AI Companion features on/off.

4. Now, click the **Account Management** tab, choose **Account Settings**, and finally choose **AI Companion**. Here, you will find account-level settings that will apply to all users in the account:

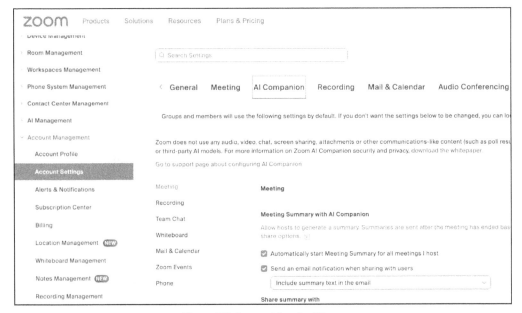

Figure 7.2: Account level settings

5. Toggle each AI Companion you would like turned on/off for the entire account. Notice that you can also lock the feature. A user will not be able to enable or disable the feature as you have locked it at an account level if you have administrator rights.

6. Finally, if you have Zoom Phone, you have additional AI Companion features you can turn on. Go to the **Zoom Phone** tab and click **AI Companion**. Choose which features you would like to enable/disable. We will dive deeper into this in the *Using AI Companion in Zoom Phone* recipe:

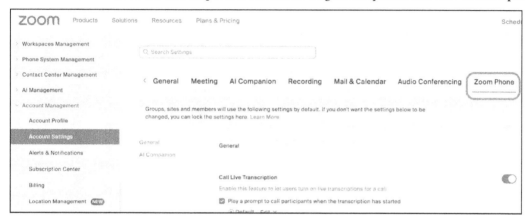

Figure 7.3: Zoom Phone

7. You're done. You now know how to enable AI Companion at a user and account level!

Using AI Companion in meetings

One of the most powerful tools when using AI Companion is that you can turn it on during meetings. This gives you two main features:

•   **Meeting summaries**: Participants can receive an AI-generated summary with the next steps of the entire meeting after the meeting ends. No more taking notes! AI Companion will create a complete recap of the meeting and send it to everyone if configured.

•   **Meeting questions**: Attendees can ask AI Companion questions based on the meeting's transcript. For example, were you 10 minutes late to the meeting? That's ok – just ask AI Companion to catch you up. You can even ask if your name was mentioned.

How to do it...

Let's explore meeting summaries and meeting questions in more detail.

Meeting summaries

Follow these steps:

1. Verify that the AI Companion meeting features that you want are turned on in your Zoom portal. As shown in *Figure 7.4*, I enabled and configured meeting summaries to automatically start and send an email summary to all meeting invitees. Adjust these settings to your needs:

> **Note**
>
> Continuing from the previous step, you could send the meeting summary to everyone who was invited. That way, if someone can't attend, they get a summary of the meeting. However, as a meeting host, you might want to control and send out the summary yourself. This is completely up to you and what works best for your needs.

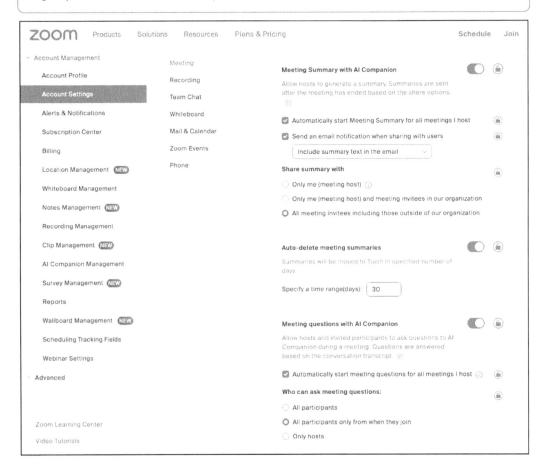

Figure 7.4: Adjusting account settings

2. In *Figure 7.4*, I checked the **Automatically start Meeting Summary for all meetings I host** box. If you leave this unchecked, users will be able to start/stop meeting summaries manually from the **Meeting Control** bar during a meeting to create a summary:

Figure 7.5: Creating summary

3. Once your meeting ends, you can decide who gets the Meeting Summary. As shown in *Figure 7.4*, I set **All meeting invitees including those outside of our organization** to receive the summary. Set the share choice to what is appropriate for your meeting. Since I have a lot of meetings with external customers, I want to share my meeting summaries with everyone who's invited every time.

4. Also, should you have enabled **Continuous Meeting Chat** for your meeting, as you learned in *Chapter 5*. By doing this, the meeting summary will be posted to your meeting channel as well:

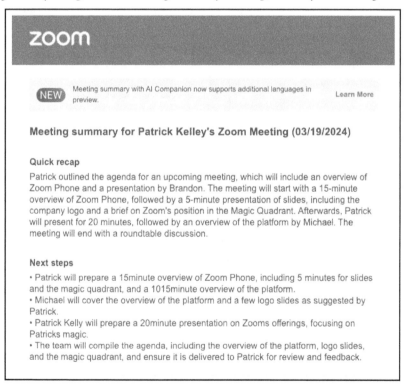

Figure 7.6: Meeting summary example

You should now be a pro at meeting summaries. AI Companion does an amazing job at summarizing the meeting (and is getting better every day), but note that like every AI model today, it sometimes gets things wrong. You should check the recording if you aren't sure it got something right.

> **Note**
>
> AI in any application isn't perfect. The more you use it, the better it gets as it learns So, always double-check spelling and grammar before sending out the meeting summary.

Meeting questions

Follow these steps:

1. Turn on **Meeting questions with AI Companion**. I configured it to **Automatically start meeting questions for all meetings I host**. If you leave this unchecked, you can manually start it from your **Meetings Control** panel during your meeting. I also configured it so that all participants can ask meeting questions. This seems like a more usable setting for the kinds of meetings I host, but choose what works best for your workflow:

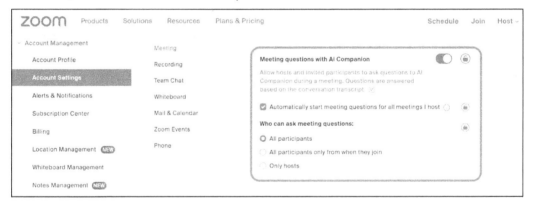

Figure 7.7: Turning on meeting questions

2. Once you start your meeting, you will now be able to ask AI Companion questions by clicking the **AI Companion** icon in your **Meetings Control** bar:

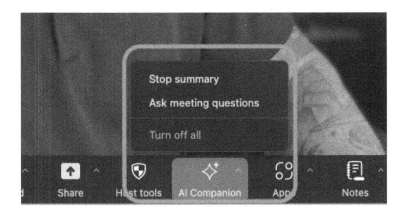

Figure 7.8: Asking questions using AI companion

3. Once you click **Ask meeting questions**, an AI Companion window will open on the right-hand side of your Zoom meeting:

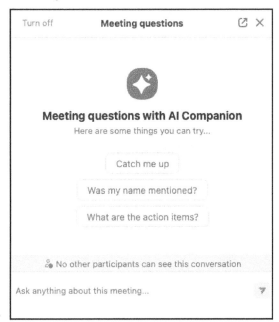

Figure 7.9: AI companion window

4. Now, you can ask AI Companion questions based on the transcript of the meeting.

> **Note**
>
> For example, if you are late to a meeting, you can ask AI Companion to **Catch me up** and you will be provided with an instant meeting summary of everything you missed. Another great use case is sometimes, I must take a call or step away from a long meeting. Once I return, I can ask AI Companion if my name was mentioned or if any action items were assigned to me.

That's it. Use meeting questions to be more productive in your next meeting!

Using AI Companion in email

Zoom integrates email into both Microsoft and Gmail. Users can seamlessly read, reply, and forward emails from within the Zoom client, as you learned in *Chapter 1*. Now, you can harness the power of AI Companion with either Microsoft or Gmail. Composing emails with AI Companion can save you time and make you more productive. No longer do you have to create an email from scratch – you can have AI Companion do this for you. What about having to type a reply to emails? You can also have AI Companion do this, giving you more time to focus on important tasks, not mundane ones.

How to do it...

Follow these steps:

1. Sign in to your Zoom portal.

2. Go to **Account Management**, choose **Account Settings**, and then click on the **AI Companion** tab. Finally, click on the **Mail & Calendar** section:

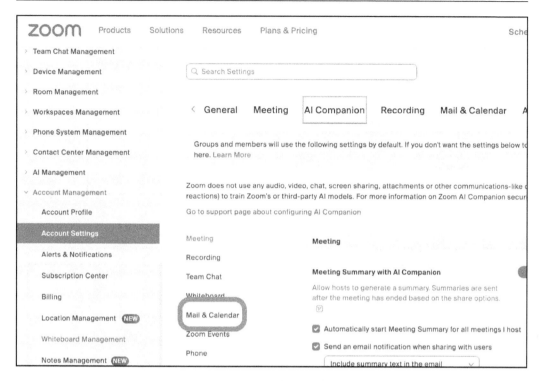

Figure 7.10: Mail & Calendar

3.   If you want to use **Email Compose with AI Companion**, toggle it on:

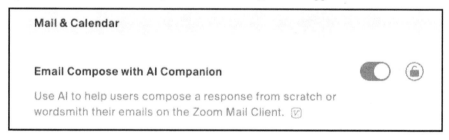

Figure 7.11: Email Compose with AI Companion

4.   Now, when you create a new email, a new **AI Companion** option will be available from your Zoom client:

Figure 7.12: AI companion in email

5.   Click on the **AI Companion** icon; a new window will appear inside your Zoom email client:

Figure 7.13: AI companion Compose

6.   You can now ask AI Companion to compose an email with any topic you want it to create. For example, you can ask AI Companion to generate an email requesting a client meeting tomorrow at 5 P.M. Once you're done, just click **Generate**:

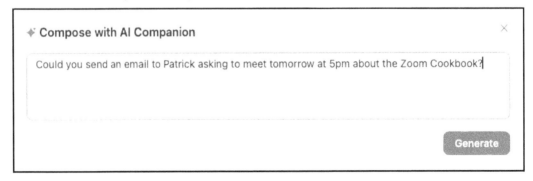

Figure 7.14: Generate button

7.   AI Companion with then create a sample email for you to review. At this point, you can tell AI Companion to make it longer or shorter or even change the tone of the email to whatever fits your needs. Click **Insert** to place the generated text in a new email:

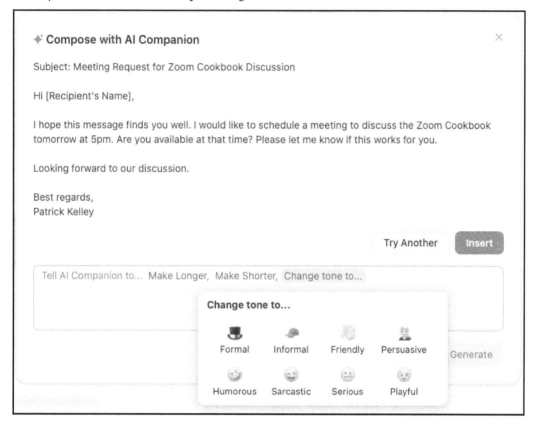

Figure 7.15: Changing tone

8.   AI Companion will now create a new email with the generated text. Just enter the email address of whomever you wish to send the email to. You can also edit the email that AI Companion composed. Once you're happy with the email, just click **Send**.

9.   AI Companion will also compose replies to emails. It works the same way as generating a new email.

10. Go to any email you've received and click **Reply** like you normally would. Instead of composing the reply yourself, ask AI Companion to do it. For example, maybe somebody asked you to attend a 5 P.M. meeting, but you can't make it. Click the **AI Companion** icon and ask AI Companion to compose a reply declining the meeting:

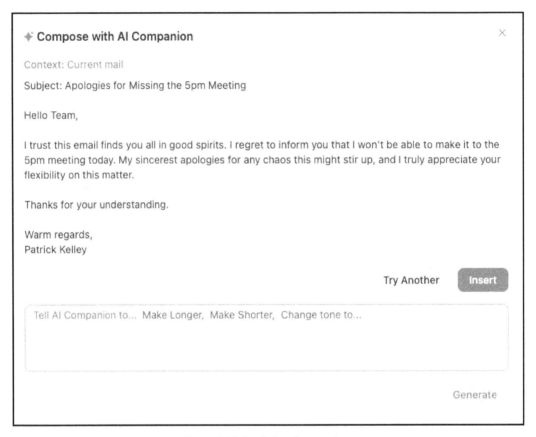

Figure 7.16: Declining the meeting

With that, you've mastered how to use emails in AI Companion!

Using AI Companion with Team Chat

Now that you've seen the power of AI Companion with email, let's apply some of what you've learned to Team Chat. You can use AI Companion to compose and reply to chats just like you learned with email, but you can also use it to summarize complete chat threads. Have you ever used Google and it uses predictive writing as you type in your search? You can use a feature called **Sentence Completion** to help you compose chats with suggestions. We will also cover **Quick Schedule**, where AI Companion can be used to detect meeting intentions and prompt you to quickly create a Zoom meeting.

How to do it...

Follow these steps:

1. Sign in to your Zoom portal.

2. Click **Account Management**, choose **Account Settings**, and then click the **AI Companion** tab. From the **AI Companion** tab, choose **Team Chat**:

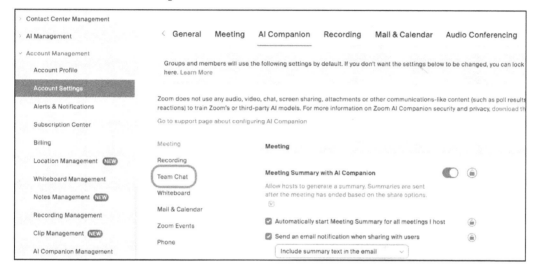

Figure 7.17: Team Chat

3. Enable all the features of AI Companion you want to activate for your account. These are account settings, so these policies will apply to all users:

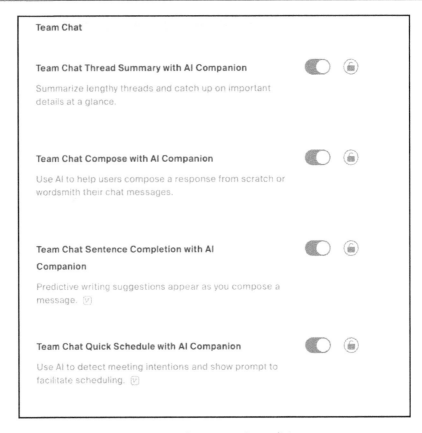

Figure 7.18: Account setting policies

In the next four recipes, we will dive into how to use all these features.

Team Chat thread summaries

Follow these steps:

1. Go to any chat thread (defined as an original chat with many replies) in Team Chat.

2. You will see that there are **9 replies** to the original chat shown in *Figure 7.18*. Next to the original chat, you will see an ellipsis as you hover over it:

Figure 7.19: Ellipses

3.   Clicking **…** will make various options will appear. Click **Summarize thread with AI Companion**:

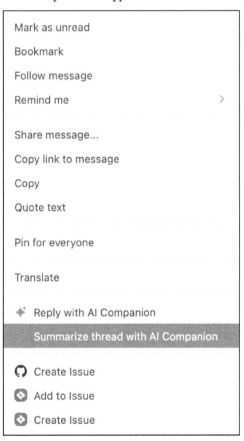

Figure 7.20: Summarize thread

4. AI Companion will now summarize the entire chat thread and produce a summary for you. Now, you don't have to read all 9 replies to quickly get caught up on the entire thread! Imagine coming back from vacation and quickly getting caught up on all the chat threads while you were out. It's a pretty cool feature:

Figure 7.21: Thread summary

Team Chat Compose

Follow these steps:

1. Much like Email Compose, you can use AI Companion to easily compose chats.

2. Go to Team Chat and start to compose a new chat or reply to an existing one. You will see an AI Companion icon once you've enabled the feature:

Figure 7.22: Icon to compose team chat

3. Click the AI Companion icon; a **Compose with AI Companion** window will appear:

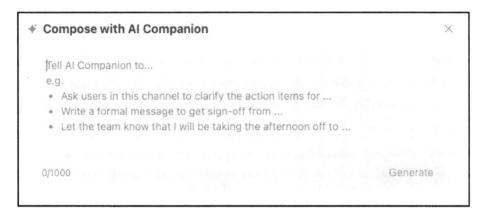

Figure 7.23: Compose with AI Companion window

4. Enter what you want AI Companion to compose. For example, there might be a long chat thread and you want everyone to understand the action items needed. Simply enter *Clarify action items* and let AI Companion generate the chat. I had AI Companion compose a chat this way; this is what it came up with. Pretty good:

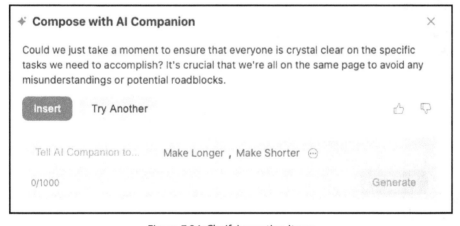

Figure 7.24: Clarifying action items

5. Just like Email Compose, you can make your chat longer or shorter and even change the tone.

6. You can edit the chat as well. When you are happy with it, you can send the chat.

With that, you're done!

Sentence Completion

Follow these steps:

1. Once you've turned this feature on in the Zoom portal, AI Companion will suggest words while a user is composing a sentence in chat. Phantom word suggestions will appear in light gray in the compose box, allowing users to accept suggestions by hitting the *Tab* button.

2. AI Companion will be able to provide real-time suggestions based on the sentence being composed, facilitating smoother and faster sentence completion for users in Team Chat. For example, I typed in "How do you think" and AI Companion suggested completing the sentence. I could accept this suggestion by clicking *Tab* or I could continue typing my sentence:

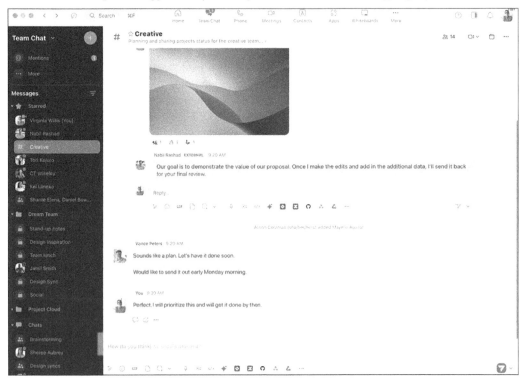

Figure 7.25: AI companion suggestions

I hope you enjoy AI Companion with Team Chat!

Quick Schedule

Follow these steps:

1. Start any chat with a user or channel and ask a question that might have a meeting suggestion. For example, in Team Chat, I asked, "*Can we meet tomorrow at 2 P.M.?*"

2. Now, AI Companion will recognize this as an intention to have a meeting at 2 P.M. tomorrow and provide a suggestion for a meeting invite:

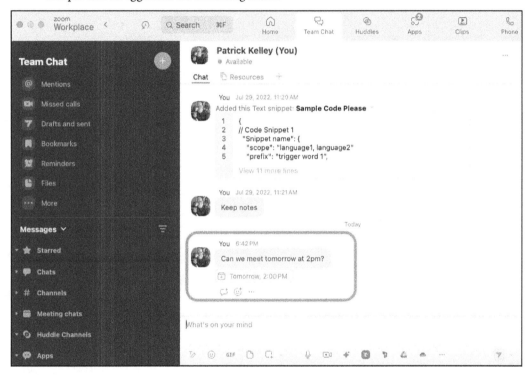

Figure 7.26: Meeting suggestion

3. Now, you can click on the meeting suggested by AI Companion and it will automatically generate a new Zoom Meeting at 2 P.M. with the person you are chatting with. That's super cool!

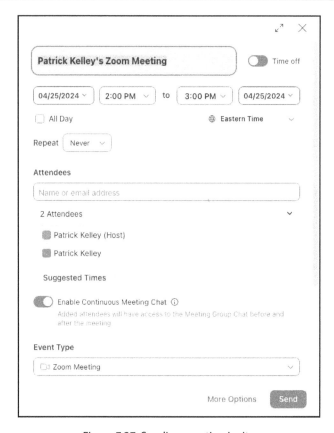

Figure 7.27: Sending meeting invite

Using AI Companion in Zoom Phone

AI Companion can also extend to Zoom Phone, creating more efficient workflows. There are four main areas that AI Companion can assist users with to become more productive:

- **Voicemail prioritization**: Allow users to prioritize voicemails based on predefined priority topics
- **Voicemail tasks**: AI Companion can quickly access a summarized list of tasks derived from your voicemail to promptly identify important items for follow-up without having to listen to the entire voicemail
- **Summarize SMS threads**: Allow users to summarize their SMS threads with AI Companion to quickly understand the conversation and generate a response (**NOTE** that this feature only applies to call queues and auto-receptionists)
- **Call summary**: There's no need to take notes anymore on a phone call – you can have AI Companion generate a summary of the call from the call transcript

How to do it...

Follow these steps:

1. Sign in to your Zoom Portal as an admin.

2. Click **Account Management**, choose **Account Settings**, and then click the **Zoom Phone** tab. Finally, click **AI Companion**:

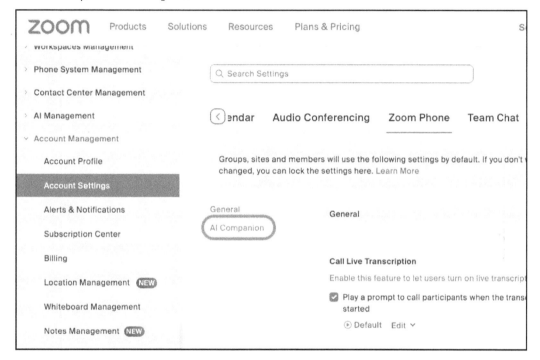

Figure 7.28: AI companion icon in Zoom Phone

3. Enable all the AI Companion features you want your users to be able to utilize. This is an account-level setting, so all Zoom Phone users will get these. Remember that you can lock them too:

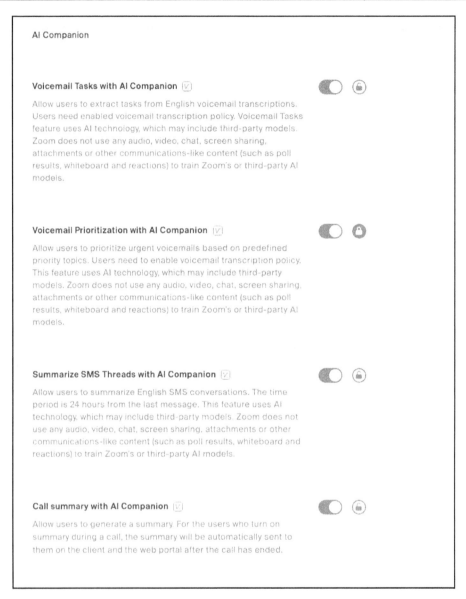

Figure 7.29: Locking the features

Voicemail prioritization

Let's take a closer look at voicemail prioritization:

1. Go to the **Settings** of your Zoom client. Then, click the **Phone** tab and scroll until you see **Voicemail prioritization with AI Companion**. Enable this feature:

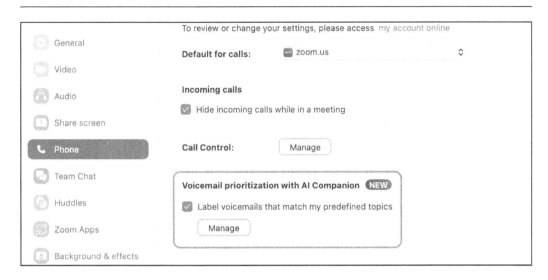

Figure 7.30: Voicemail prioritization

2. Now, click **Manage** to add predefined topics. A new window will appear Click **Add** to enter your topic. You can add up to five topics. The topic is limited to 50 characters or less:

Figure 7.31: Adding priority topic

3. AI Companion will enter a description that matches your topic. Approve or edit this description to ensure it closely matches your topic, then click **Approve and submit**. Take a look at *Figure 7.32*. Here, you can see an example definition for *Billing Classification*:

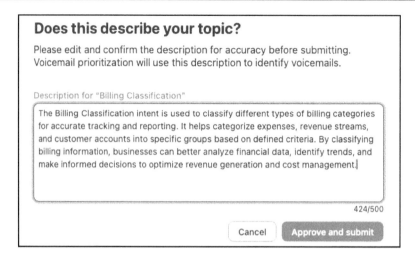

Figure 7.32: Billing Classification

4. Now, when you receive a voicemail that matches your prioritization topics, it will be highlighted with the keywords that match your topic. This will allow you to easily prioritize which voicemails are important and you can quickly filter which ones to listen to first. In *Figure 7.33*, I have two voicemails that match my topics:

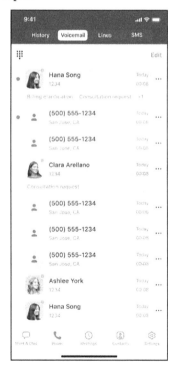

Figure 7.33: Filtering voicemails

5.   With that, you've mastered voicemail prioritization!

Voicemail tasks

Let's look at voicemail tasks in more depth:

1.   To use AI Companion to determine any tasks from a voicemail, go to **Zoom Phone** and click on the **Voicemail** tab.

2.   Go to any voicemail, then click on the AI Companion **View Task** icon:

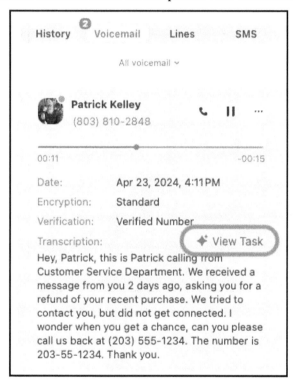

Figure 7.34: View task

3.   AI Companion will now review the transcript of the voicemail and display the tasks that it extracted. *Figure 7.35* shows that I need to call Patrick back about my refund:

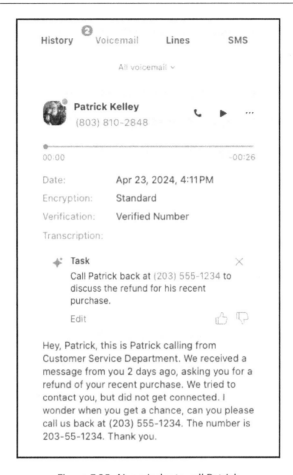

Figure 7.35: Ai reminder to call Patrick

Great – you know how to use voicemail tasks!

Summarizing SMS threads

Follow these steps to learn how to summarize SMS threads:

1. Click the **Phone** tab in your Zoom client.

2. Click the **SMS** tab.

3. In the text box, click the **Summarize with AI Companion** icon.

4. A summary of the SMS thread will appear:

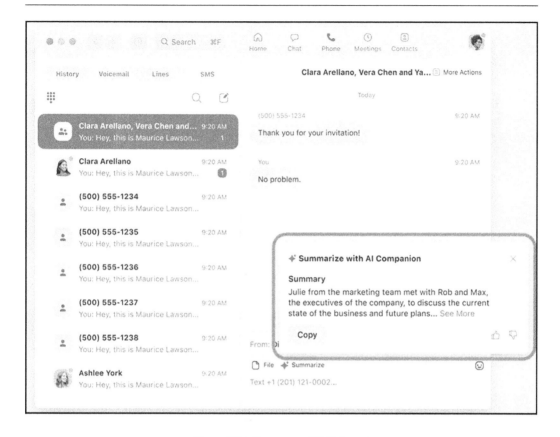

Figure 7.36: Summary of SMS thread

That's it! Pretty simple right?

Call summary

Finally, let's look at how to generate a call summary:

1. While on a Zoom Phone call, click the **Summarize** icon to initiate a call summary:

Figure 7.37: Summarize icon

2. A visual prompt will appear to turn call summary on (**Summarize** in *Figure 7.39*). Once turned on, an audio prompt will be heard, letting the parties know that the call is being summarized.

3. You can also stop the summary at any time during the call.

4. After the call is complete, AI Companion will generate a call summary.

5. To view all summaries, click the **History** tab. Then, under the **All History** filter, select **Summary**.

6. Find the call you wish to review and click the **Summary** icon. The AI Companion summary window will expand:

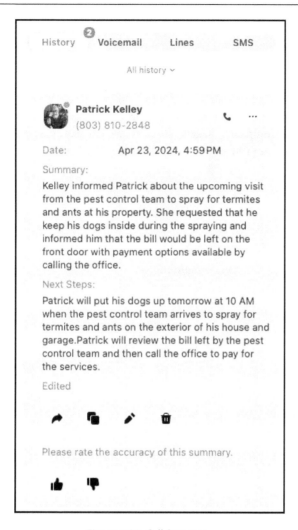

Figure 7.38: Call Summary

7. As shown in *Figure 7.38*, AI Companion generated a summary of the phone call and created the next steps for the participants. It's a great way to no longer take notes during a phone call. Let AI Companion do it for you!

8. You can now click the **Forward** button to send the summary via email to anyone who might benefit from it.

9. You can also **Copy** the summary to a clipboard and paste it where needed, such as a chat with a co-worker.

10. You can click the **Edit** button to edit the summary for any mispronunciation of words or names.

11. You can also rate the accuracy of the summary to give feedback to AI Companion.

Enjoy using call summary!

Using AI Companion in Whiteboard

You can leverage AI Companion to generate Zoom Whiteboard content. The hardest part about whiteboards to me is a blank whiteboard. I always have a creative block regarding visual ideas. Fortunately, you can use AI Companion to generate creative whiteboards, as well as create ideas, refine and extend existing content, or even add new content using AI Companion.

How to do it...

Follow these steps:

1. Create or open an existing whiteboard.

2. In the left toolbar, click the **AI Companion** icon:

Figure 7.39: AI Companion icon in Whiteboard

3. The **Whiteboard Content Generation** window will appear.

4. Enter your criteria for generating content. It could be anything. For example, say you want AI Companion to generate content on dinosaurs. In this case, you could type "*What are the most popular dinosaurs?*"

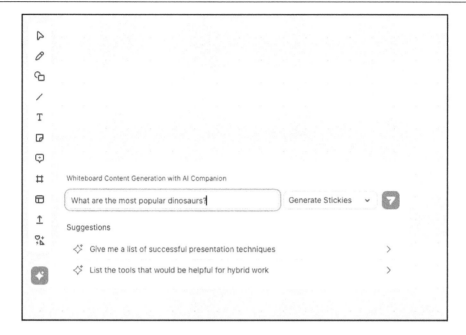

Figure 7.40: Prompt

5. Now choose what type of content you want AI Companion to create. Click the drop-down menu to the right of your input prompt. Here, you can choose how you want your idea to be created. I am going to choose **Generate Stickies**:

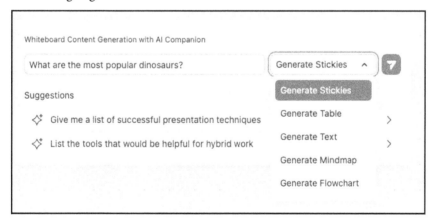

Figure 7.41: Generate stickers

6. AI Companion will now generate a whiteboard with your content using stickies. It did a pretty good job. Check it out!

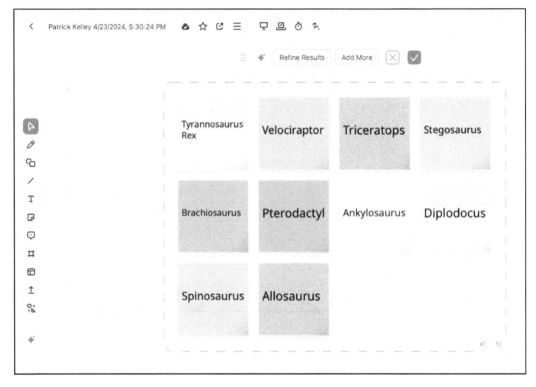

Figure 7.42: Stickies

7. You can ask AI Companion to refine the results or add more stickies. This is your whiteboard, so feel free to edit it however you want. Once you're happy with the result, click the checkmark icon. AI Companion's job is to help you be more creative!

8. Remember, whiteboards are not static. They can be as large as you need. What if I also wanted to create a whiteboard for a presentation and I needed some ideas on how to tell my story better? You can ask AI Companion to generate a table with successful presentation techniques. Look at the result!

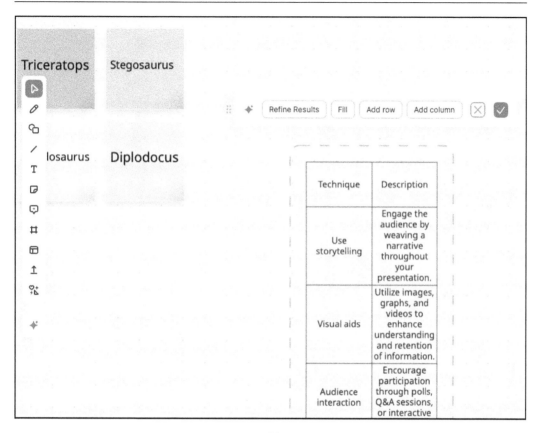

Figure 7.43: Table generation

9. Again, you can edit your table however you want. Add a new row or column if you need to.

10. I hope you have seen how powerful AI Companion can be when it comes to generating creative whiteboard ideas. Try it out!

8
Security and Privacy

Zoom places a great deal of emphasis on security, safety, privacy, and compliance. In the last few years, Zoom has developed a number of features that should instill a great deal of trust in its platform. Zoom enables users at all levels from commercial to full enterprise-level usage to secure every level of their collaboration and communication platform. We are going to present an overview of the main features you can utilize to increase security and privacy with the main modalities within Zoom that you have learned from previous chapters. This is by no means an exhaustive list as there are literally thousands of ways to enhance Zoom security, privacy, and safety within its verbose platform. Zoom places a lot of time and effort into compliance, for example. Meeting standards such as ISO certifications, **Health Insurance Portability and Accountability Act (HIPPA)** compliance, and the **Federal Risk and Authorization Management Program (FedRAMP)** is great, but I want to keep this chapter relevant to everyday users like you. Therefore I want to spend our time on how to implement features and functions that make a difference and the use cases associated with them. I also want to educate you on the Zoom security features that will instill confidence in the platform. I also want to give you a number of resources that you can dive deeper into if you want to learn even more about Zoom security, compliance, and privacy.

In this chapter, we're going to cover the following main topics:

- Protecting Zoom from the portal
- Securing Zoom from the client

Protecting Zoom from the portal

As a Zoom meeting or webinar host, you have several features to protect your meetings and webinars. Let's explore some of these features and how and why you would use them. Zoom has dozens of security features, and we won't dive deep into all of them as it's an exhaustive list. We will cover the most useful ones, but I will give you resources should you need to secure and protect your meetings even further.

How to do it...

1. Sign in to the Zoom portal.

2. Navigate to **Settings**, then click the **Meetings** tab, then click **Security**. We will now go down the list of all relevant options for you to implement:

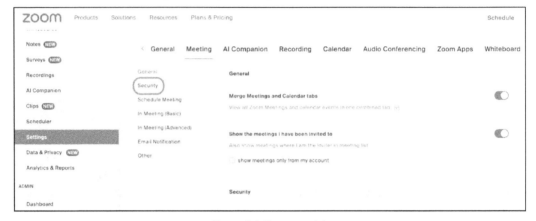

Figure 8.1: Zoom portal

3. You'll notice that at least one security option is required for all Zoom meetings. This will either be a passcode, waiting room, or authentication. By default, if none of the options are selected, Zoom will implement waiting rooms:

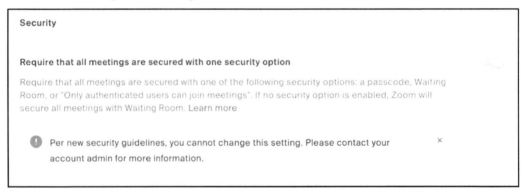

Figure 8.2: Security options

4. Waiting rooms are an effective way to screen who is trying to enter your Zoom session and keep unwanted guests out. Waiting rooms will require all participants to be placed in a waiting room, and then the host will need to manually admit each invitee individually. As a host, you will have complete control over who you admit to a meeting. You also will be able to edit waiting room options, such as everyone going into a waiting room or users not in your account. You can also allow all users who were invited to the meeting to bypass the waiting room.

To get started, click the **Edit Options** link to adjust these settings. You can also customize your waiting room with logos, branding, and even custom videos while users wait. Click the **Customize Waiting Room** link to apply the features needed. This is a great feature should you have a lot of public meetings that may be published on social media or websites, and you want to control who is admitted. This prevents people joining your meeting who you don't recognize:

Waiting Room

When participants join a meeting, place them in a waiting room and require the host to admit them individually. Enabling the waiting room automatically disables the setting for allowing participants to join before host.

Waiting Room Options

The options you select here apply to meetings hosted by users who turned 'Waiting Room' on

✓ Everyone will go in the waiting room

✓ People in the waiting room are sorted by join order

Edit Options Customize Waiting Room

Figure 8.3: Waiting Room

5. You also can apply *meeting passcodes*. Therefore, any ad hoc or scheduled Zoom meeting will require an invitee to enter the proper passcode before admittance into the meeting. Zoom will create a random passcode when creating a meeting, and all meeting participants will be required to enter the proper passcode before being admitted to the meeting. This is a great feature when you send out Zoom meeting invitations to a big group and you don't want to manually admit users with the **Waiting Room** feature. This way, only invitees will know the passcode (*FYI*: You can also apply the **Waiting Room** feature and passcode in unison for extra security):

Meeting Passcode

All instant, and scheduled meetings that users can join via client, or room systems will be passcode-protected. The Personal Meeting ID (PMI) meetings are not included.

Figure 8.4: Meeting passcode

6. Zoom also has a **Personal Meeting ID** or **PMI** passcode option. This is a passcode that you can choose to apply to all Zoom meetings that are static and always the same. All your meetings created will have the same PMI instead of a randomly generated passcode. This isn't as secure as meeting passcodes, but you can change your PMI at any time as well. Use this sparingly with only people you know and trust. If you question which method to use, use waiting rooms or passcodes before you share your PMI:

Personal Meeting ID (PMI) Passcode

All Personal Meeting ID (PMI) meetings that users can join via client, or room systems will be passcode-protected.

Passcode: ****** Show Edit

Figure 8.5: PMI

7. You can also generate passcodes for webinars should you need an extra layer of security. Recall from *Chapter 6, Zoom Webinars,* that you can require all attendees to register before a meeting, so use the passcodes-in-webinars feature carefully as it increases friction for all webinar attendees, but it certainly can add another security layer should you require it:

Webinar Passcode

A passcode will be generated when scheduling a Webinar and participants require the passcode to join the Webinar.

Figure 8.6: Webinar passcode

8. A great feature I always use is embedding the passcode into the Zoom invite. This way, users who were specifically invited to the meeting will have an invite link that already has the passcode embedded in their invite link and won't need to manually enter the passcode. All others will need to manually enter the passcode. This helps apply security to your Zoom meeting without causing friction with your invited users:

Embed passcode in invite link for one-click join

Meeting passcode will be encrypted and included in the invite link to allow participants to join with just one click without having to enter the passcode.

Figure 8.7: Embedded passcode

9. Requiring all webinar panelists to authenticate before joining a webinar is a great way to secure your next Zoom webinar. I highly encourage you to enable this feature (*Note*: More on this feature in the next recipe.):

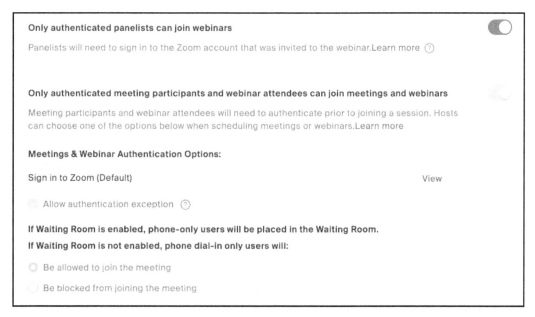

Figure 8.8: Webinar authentication

10. I would also recommend you require all users using the Zoom web client to authenticate before being able to join your Zoom meeting to prevent any unwanted attendees from being able to join your meeting from any browser. If you don't implement this feature, anyone can join your Zoom session without the need for a Zoom client or an account:

Figure 8.9: Web client

11. Zoom has advanced security and encryption features should you need **end-to-end encryption** (**E2EE**). I would only use this feature for meetings that require the utmost security. For example, if I were having a meeting about a company acquisition or employee salaries, I would probably use E2EE. This feature does limit modalities such as meeting recordings or phone dial-in, so only use this security level when needed:

> **Note**
> Notice how I applied this feature at the account level and then locked it (as you learned how to do in previous chapters) because it is grayed out without the ability to turn it off.

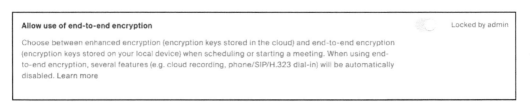

Figure 8.10: E2EE

12. For security reasons, it's probably a good idea to not allow attendees to record the meeting locally on their local computer unless there is a specific need to do so. For example, I use a third-party editor sometimes, and it's easier to use a local recording file instead of a cloud recording. I use **Cloud Recordings** and then share the recording as needed, which keeps the recording secure in the Zoom cloud with encryption. However, use what works best for your workflow. You have the option to toggle local recordings on or off.

In your Zoom portal, go to **Settings** then click **Recording**. Navigate to **Local recording** and toggle this feature on or off:

Figure 8.11: Local recording

13. Turning off file transfer in meetings or webinars is also a good best practice for bigger meetings or webinars with many attendees you aren't familiar with, such as in a public forum. I typically leave file transfer on as I mainly have smaller meetings where I need this feature to share files. Choose which option works best for you. It's also worth mentioning that it's best practice to send links to files instead of the actual file itself. For example, I've seen companies turn off file transfer altogether. This then forces users to send links to files in protected file repositories such as Google Drive, OneDrive, or Box.

To enable/disable the file transfer feature, go to your Zoom portal and click **Settings**, then click **Meeting** and scroll down until you see **Send files via meeting chat** and **Send files via webinar chat**. Toggle each on or off depending on your security needs. You can also limit what kinds of files can be sent, as well as file size:

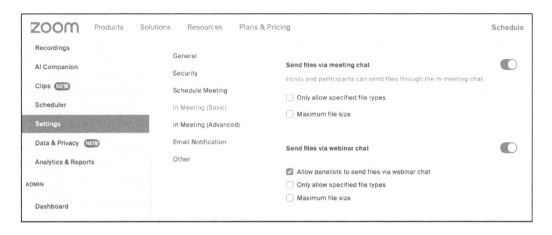

Figure 8.12: File transfer

14. By default, all Zoom meetings and webinars are fully encrypted on many levels. I don't want this to get too nerdy, but here is a quick overview:

- **TLS**: All connections between your Zoom client and Zoom's cloud use TLS 1.2 encryption and **public key infrastructure** (**PKI**) certificates. This basically means that everything you do in Zoom uses high encryption levels for communication.

- **AES**: Zoom uses 256-bit AES-**Galois/Counter Mode** (**GCM**) encryption mode for all data streams. Basically, Zoom uses high encryption technology to make sure all your video, voice, and shared content is ultra-secure.

- **SRTP**: This fancy acronym that means Zoom Phone also uses AES-256 GCM to encrypt and protect all phone conversations.

- **E2EE**: All data between meeting participants is known only to the devices of those participants. This ensures that no third parties (even Zoom) have access to any meeting data.

The aforementioned are the most commonly used security features you can set at an administrative level for Zoom. There are many more, but these should get you started and fit almost any workflow. To learn how to secure Zoom even further, please ensure you read the last recipe in this chapter.

Securing your Zoom webinars further

Please go back to *Chapter 6*, to the *Setting up registration* recipe, in which I dove deep into the different methodologies of Zoom registration for webinars. This is vital information in learning how to implement proper security into your webinars with registration techniques. Review the aforementioned recipe to enable registration in your webinar for added security, then come back to learn more!

Let's learn some additional layers of security to apply to your webinars as well:

1. Create or edit a Zoom webinar from the Zoom portal.

2. Navigate to the **Authentication** section:

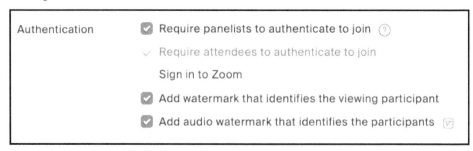

Figure 8.13: Authentication

3. Please toggle **Require panelists to authenticate to join**. This is obvious, but this requires all panelists to authenticate with the account that was used to invite them to the webinar. Therefore, all panelists and or co-hosts will have to have a Zoom account.

4. Also, you can toggle **Require attendees to authenticate to join**. As you can see, because I made this an account-level setting, this is required for all users because it is grayed out. You learned how to lock settings in previous recipes. This setting requires all attendees to authenticate before joining a webinar for an extra layer of security, but use this feature with a bit of caution for large webinars where attendees might not have a Zoom account and just want to view the webinar. For example, say you are selling a product or service and want as many attendees as possible. You wouldn't want to create a lot of friction for people to join.

5. You can also enable **Add watermark that identifies the viewing participant**. This feature superimposes an image, consisting of a participant's email address, onto the shared content they are viewing over their video. This feature ensures that shared or confidential information is labeled should someone share the screen or recording elsewhere inappropriately, allowing you to easily identify the person.

6. Also, toggle on **Add audio watermark that identifies the participants**. This then adds an audio signature to the webinar or meeting. This is an inaudible watermark of a user's personal information embedded in the audio that is played through the receiving user's speakers by the client receiving the audio from Zoom. This means that if someone records the webinar or meeting with a separate microphone or third-party software and then shares the audio file without permission, Zoom can assist with determining which participant was responsible.

I told you Zoom was great at security!

Securing Zoom from the client

All the additional security features until now have been set from the Zoom portal. There are many additional in-meeting features that you can utilize directly from the Zoom client in real time during your meetings and webinars.

How to do it...

1. Start or join any Zoom meeting/webinar as the host.

2. As a host, you will have control of your attendees with several Zoom security features. Click the **Participants** icon in your *meeting control* bar. All participants in your meeting will appear in the **Participants** window to the right of your video feed (*Note*: Webinars will have attendees, panelists, and/or co-hosts):

Figure 8.14: Participants icon

3. Now, you can hover over any participant and control their audio by muting them. Hosts cannot unmute someone, only mute. For example, there might be a situation during a meeting where an attendee might be saying something controversial or inappropriate that you don't want or need your attendees to hear. Click the **Mute** button to turn off their audio. This use case might be a bit extreme for the sake of an example. Most likely, you will use this feature when someone forgets their mic is on and might be in a noisy environment or having a side conversation that is disturbing the meeting. As a host, you can easily mute their mic. Panelists also have the ability to unmute themselves at a later time should they need to speak during the meeting:

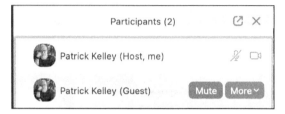

Figure 8.15: Mute

4. If you click the **More** button from *Figure 8.15*, you will see some additional security features you can use as a host. Let's review them next.

5. Just as with muting a participant's audio, you can also stop their video feed. For example, an attendee might be showing inappropriate footage from their video feed that is disruptive to the meeting or holding up disruptive signs or banners. Click **Stop video** and their camera feed will be turned off:

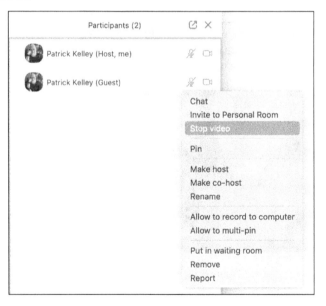

Figure 8.16: Stop video

6. As an added layer of security, the attendees will be unable to restart their video feed unless you as host allow them to. They will receive a notification that they can't start their video if they attempt to turn it back on:

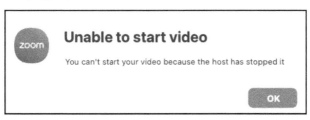

Figure 8.17: Stopped video notification

7. Should you as the host want to allow them to start their video again during the meeting, you can click **Ask to start video**, and the attendees will get a notification that they can once again start their video:

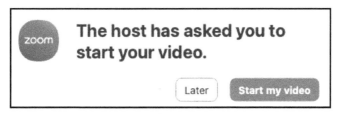

Figure 8.18: Start video notification

8. An additional feature that can be used from the Zoom client is to place disruptive attendees into a waiting room. This will move such attendees from the meeting into your waiting room. The attendees will no longer have the ability to share audio or video or present anything during the meeting, nor will they be able to view the meeting. They will also not be able to chat with any hosts or attendees:

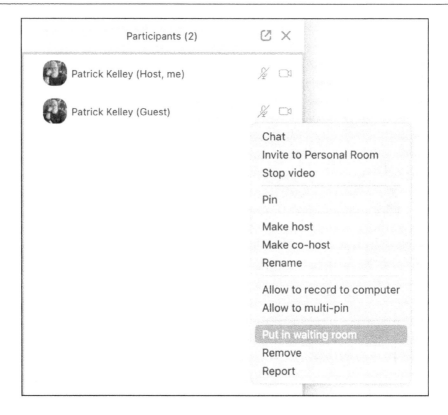

Figure 8.19: Waiting room

9. As a host, you can send messages to the waiting room for attendees to read by clicking the **Message** link, but they will not be able to respond. You can also admit them back into the meeting at any time by clicking the **Admit** button:

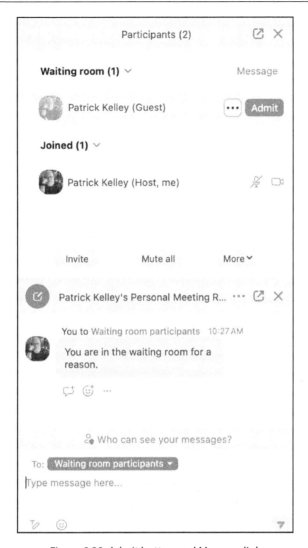

Figure 8.20: Admit button and Message link

10. A more severe security measure you can use as a host is to remove an attendee from the meeting entirely by clicking the **Remove** button. This would be used in a situation where you no longer wish the attendee to return because of their disruptive or inappropriate behavior. You can also configure the ability for the attendee to return to the meeting. More on that in *step 12*:

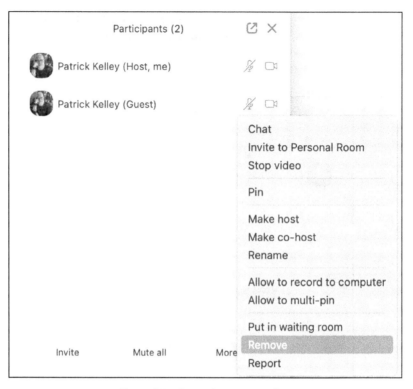

Figure 8.21: Removing an attendee

11. A drastic feature that can be used by the host for participants is the **Report** feature. By clicking **Report**, users will then be removed from the meeting, and their behavior will be reported to Zoom. Zoom will then use the meeting information (with your consent) to investigate the reported attendee. For example, proper use of reporting a meeting attendee is if a user is impersonating another individual or perhaps using copyright or trademarked information or offensive and abusive behavior:

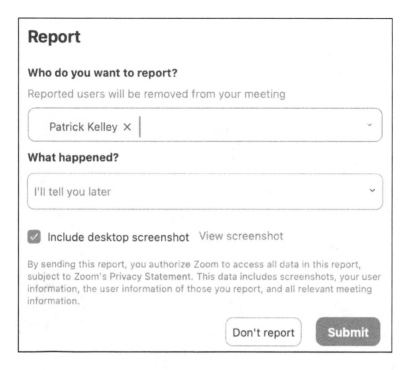

Figure 8.22: Reporting an attendee

12. An even greater level of security you may wish to employ is to set a feature that ensures any removed participants are unable to rejoin the meeting.

Go back to your *Zoom admin*, click **Account Management**, then **Account Settings**. Scroll until you see the **Allow removed participants to rejoin** setting. Verify this is toggled off. Any previously removed meeting or webinar panelists will be unable to rejoin the meeting. Since as a host, you removed the attendee/panelist for a very valid reason, not allowing them back into the meeting is probably a good idea:

Figure 8.23: Zoom admin setting

13. Finally, from the Zoom client, you can lock a meeting. Locking a meeting stops any new attendees who aren't already in the meeting from joining. For example, say you invited 10 people to attend your meeting, and all 10 have joined. At this point, you can lock the meeting, preventing any further attendees from joining as they wouldn't have been invited nor are expected.

Click the **Host tools** icon in your *meeting control* bar. A list of options will appear. Click the **Lock Meeting** feature. Your meeting will now be locked, and no new attendees will be able to join. You can later unlock the meeting if you wish as well, for new attendees to join:

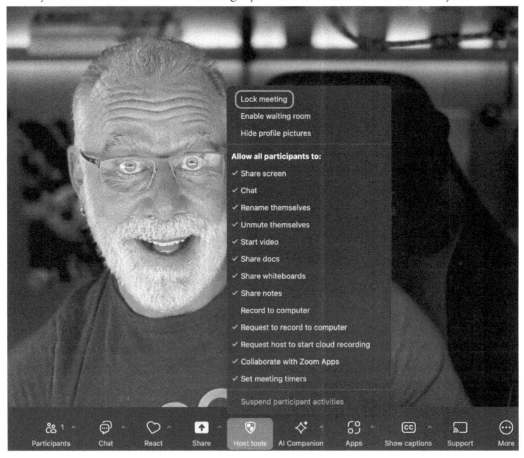

Figure 8.24: Lock meeting

14. The most extreme security feature that a host can use is **Suspend participant activities**. This basically shuts down the entire meeting. Everyone will be muted, video and screen sharing will be stopped, breakout rooms will be closed, all Zoom apps will be disabled, and the entire meeting will be locked. You also will have the option to report the meeting to Zoom for further investigation. This is a pretty drastic measure and should only be used in dire situations. You can see from *Figure 8.24* that this option is highlighted in red to let you know visually the importance of using this step:

Figure 8.25: Suspending a meeting

15. You learned sharing options in *Chapter 2*, but recall you can control who gets to share during a meeting by clicking on the ^ sign next to the **Share** icon in your *meetings control* bar. For public meetings where you might not know all the attendees, use the **Host Only** feature to limit random people from sharing during your meeting. You can change this feature at any time. I typically use the **All participants** sharing option, but my meetings are smaller, and I know everyone most of the time, so pick the feature that fits your workflow:

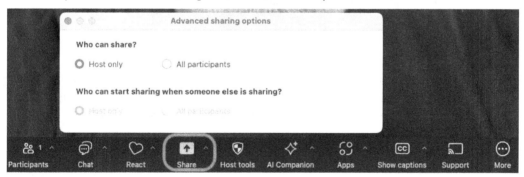

Figure 8.26: Sharing options

16. You learned how to use annotations in *Chapter 2*. You can control who has permission to annotate on your screen share. By default, everyone can annotate, but you may wish to control this. For example, in large public meetings, you don't want a bunch of attendees annotating on important presentation. Or, maybe you're a teacher in a virtual classroom and don't want your students writing on the screen during a lesson. In those situations, it would be helpful to disable their ability to annotate.

During your screen share, navigate to your *meeting control* bar and click **...** for **More** options. Then, click **Disable annotation for others** if you don't want meeting attendees annotating during your screen share:

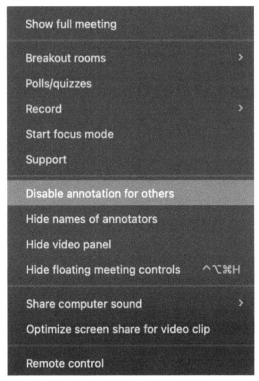

Figure 8.27: Annotation controls

17. As the host, you can also limit in-meeting chats if you choose to increase security for more public or large meetings when you don't know the attendees well or what they might send to everyone. Perhaps you want to limit distractions such as a bunch of chats during the meeting or webinar.

    Click the **Chat** icon in your *meeting control* bar. Then, click the ellipsis (**...**) in the chat window. You can choose who participants can chat with, if at all:

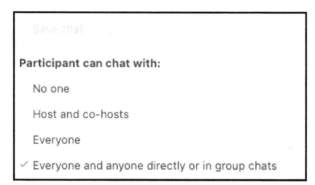

Figure 8.28: In-meeting chat

As you can see, Zoom takes security seriously and gives you a lot of tools to use from both the portal and the client. Happy Zooming.

Diving deeper into security, privacy, and compliance

This cookbook is focused on creating recipes that allow you as an admin or user to make the most out of your Zoom experience with features and modalities. You can implement many more features in Zoom with security, privacy, and compliance. Many of these are out of the scope of this cookbook, but I wanted to at least arm you with additional information that will allow you to dive much deeper into these topics if you wish. For example, Zoom has the ability to enforce policies that can block specific domains or even geographic regions. You can enforce passcode complexity requirements or define keywords and text patterns for chat compliance. You can also integrate Zoom with companies such as Okta, Microsoft, Theta Lake, and so on to enforce granular levels of privacy, security, and compliance as well. All of these are out of the scope of a cookbook but are options available to you to increase Zoom platform security even further.

9

Advanced Tips and Tricks

In the previous eight chapters, we have dove deep into many of the everyday features that you can utilize from the **Zoom** platform. In this chapter, I want to concentrate on some of the more advanced features that Zoom offers. These are features that most likely have specific use cases that might not apply to the everyday user, but certainly have a place when using Zoom. All these advanced features are compartmentalized, meaning that they don't necessarily relate to each other in any way but are more advanced features that can be used to be more productive and efficient as a user. Some features are add-ons to features you've already learned. Basically, each of the recipes that we will discuss in this chapter will expand your knowledge of Zoom even further, allowing you to take complete advantage of the entire platform. I know that might sound a little vague, but you will understand how these features can fit into your workflows as you go through this chapter.

In this chapter, we're going to cover the following main topics:

- Using **Smart Recording**
- Using **Zoom Clips**
- Using **Zoom Huddles**
- Streaming Zoom to social media
- Using **Zoom Apps**
- Using avatars and filters
- Using a secondary camera
- Enhancing video quality
- Improving audio quality

Using Smart Recording

Smart Recording allows hosts to get more out of the Zoom meetings and webinars with **AI Companion**. Smart Recording allows AI Companion to automatically divide your cloud recordings into smart chapters for easy reviewing. It also highlights important information and creates the next steps for actionable items. Smart Recording also provides valuable analytics to the host with things such as conversation factors, talk speed, talk-listen ratio, longest talk monologues, filler words, and even patience.

The main purpose of Smart Recording is to be more efficient and effective when watching a recording. Have you ever watched a 45-meeting recording and at the end of it thought, "That was a waste of my time. My name wasn't mentioned nor were there any action items for me to work on." Smart Recording can help. Imagine watching a recording and you could search for your name quickly from the meeting transcript and jump to that part of the recording. What if there were already action items created that you could quickly review to see if you need to work on something assigned to you? You could quickly review meeting analytics to see if you talked too much and didn't listen enough or maybe even talked faster than you should. You could use that data to become a better presenter or salesperson. That is the power of Smart Recording.

How to do it...

Enable Smart Recording

Follow these steps to enable Smart Recording:

1. First, you need to enable Smart Recording. You can do this for a user, group, or entire account if you want.

    To enable per user, sign in to your Zoom portal.

2. In the navigation menu, click **Settings**, then click the **AI Companion** tab, and then click the **Recording** section.

    Now, toggle on **Smart Recording with AI Companion**.

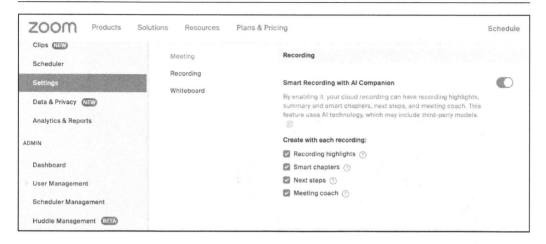

Figure 9.1: Smart Recording

With each Smart Recording, you can enable one or all features of the four available. I suggest you turn them all on for the greatest benefit. You can hover over the **?** symbol next to the specific feature to learn more. Here are those four features:

- **Recording highlights**: Meeting details in the audio transcript will be highlighted. Hosts can modify highlighted sections and even create a video summary.

- **Smart Chapters**: You're recording will have chapter overviews. The host can also edit these as well.

- **Next steps**: A summary of action items will be created after the meeting.

- **Meeting coach**: This creates speaker metrics such as talk-listen ratio, talk speed, filler words, and longest spiel. Users can view their own metrics; admins will be able to view them all.

Since you have now enabled Smart Recording, the next time you record a meeting/webinar to the cloud, it will be turned on.

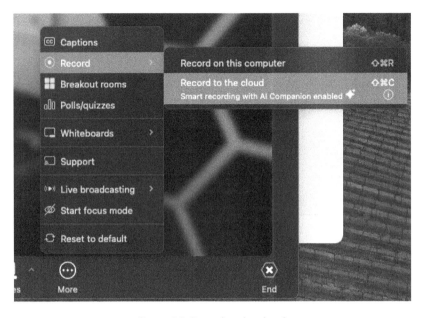

Figure 9.2: Record to the cloud

3.   To view your Smart Recordings, go to your Zoom portal.

Click **Recordings** and then you will see your Zoom recordings and Smart Recordings listed in the **Cloud Recordings** tab.

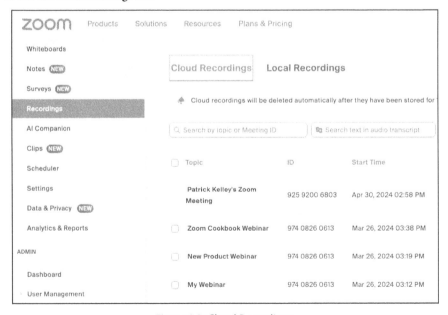

Figure 9.3: Cloud Recordings

Creating recording highlights

Here are the steps for creating recording highlights:

1. Once you open your Smart Recordings, you will see the audio transcript and recording highlights.

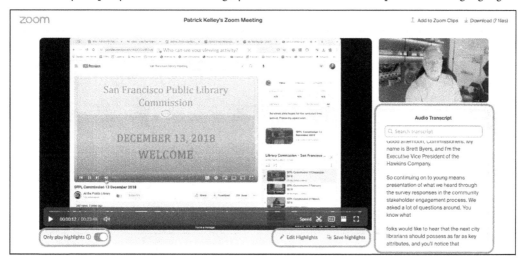

Figure 9.4: Highlights

2. You can search the entire transcript for important details during the meeting or even your name to see whether there were tasks assigned to you.

3. You can edit the transcript, such as renaming a speaker or editing misspelled words or acronyms, by hovering over the transcript and clicking the edit pencil.

4. You can also highlight specific paragraphs by hovering over them and clicking the highlight icon.

5. You can even add/remove the highlights in the video by clicking **Edit Highlights**.

6. Users can also play just the highlights of the meeting by using the **Only play highlights** option.

7. A powerful feature is the **Save highlights** option. This will save only the highlights of the meeting into a separate recording. You can create a 5-minute video of highlights instead of having users watch an entire 30-minute video recording.

Smart chapters

1. Scroll down and you will see a **Summary and smart chapters** tab.

Figure 9.5: Smart chapters

2. AI Companion will create a summary of the entire meeting.

3. AI Companion will also split the meeting up into smart chapters and create a summary of each chapter. Hover over each chapter to read a summary of that specific chapter.

4. You can also edit the smart chapter title as well as the summary text by hovering over it and clicking **Edit Smart Chapters**.

Next Steps

1. To the right of **Smart Chapters**, you will see **Next Steps**.

Figure 9.6: Next Steps

2. AI Companion will create any next steps from the meeting transcript.

3. If you hover over **Next Steps**, you can edit the text as well.

My meeting coach

1. **Click** the **My meeting coach** tab:

Figure 9.7: My meeting coach

2. In this section, you will see the metrics of your meeting. Hover over each metric to learn more about what each metric means and the score of how your meeting went based on predefined ranges.

3. You can now review and share more than just a full recording of your last meeting or webinar, which helps you focus on improving your speaking abilities for future meetings.

Using Zoom Clips

You learned how to use video messages in *Chapter 2*. Take it to the next level with Zoom Clips. Easily record, edit, and share high-fidelity short-form video messages both internally and externally. Help teams to communicate asynchronously, reduce Zoom meetings, and cut down on lost time due to ambiguous communication. Read that part again – *actually* reduce the time you spend in meetings!

Zoom Clips allows users to record their video and screen to share with others, and even store clips in a content management system for simple search and discovery to promote team engagement. Team members can even comment on videos and creators can track views.

Zoom Clips is an extension to asynchronous communication tools that users can utilize to work flexibly and when they want. Zoom Clips allows workers to provide project updates, deliver training, and even uplevel new hires for a frictionless experience. Imagine sending a video demo or a product walk-through without having a meeting. Then, recipients can comment and react to your clip to keep the conversation constructive and ongoing without having to schedule an hour-long meeting, saving time and effort in the process.

How to do it...

Manage Zoom Clips

1. First, you must enable Zoom Clips.

2. Sign into the Zoom portal. Click **Settings** and then click the **Clips** tab.

3. Toggle the **Clips** feature on.

4. Choose whether to **Allow users who can access clips to download clips**. I don't really enable this feature as I want to keep all videos in a single repository, and you also lose the ability to track views.

5. Toggle on **Viewers can view comments** as well. Enabling these features adds to the overall user experience, in my opinion.

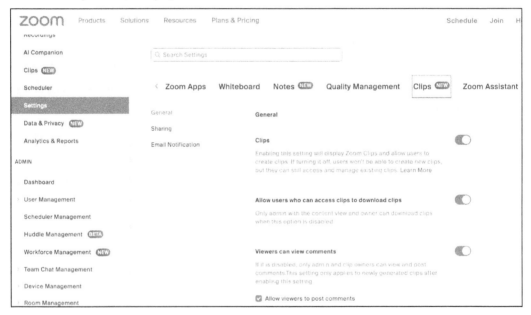

Figure 9.8: Zoom Clips

6. Configure how you would like to share clips. I typically choose **Anyone with the link** for more useability, but you can limit access if you have security concerns. This can be adjusted per clip as well. For example, you may have clips that you only want people in your account or company able to access; in this case, you can configure each clip individually.

7. I also don't require a passcode for my clips, but you can enable a random passcode to be generated, and users are required to enter it before viewing your clip if you feel the need.

8. I always toggle on **Display the shared clip's thumbnail, title, and description** so users can quickly view the relevance of your created clip.

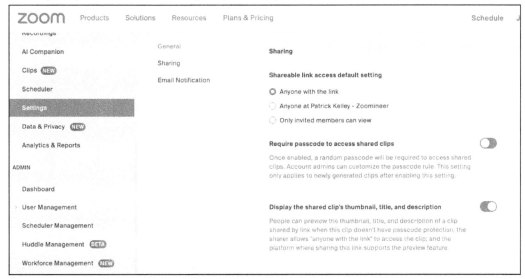

Figure 9.9: Sharing clips

10. You can also set email notifications with clips.

11. By default, all are toggled on but choose which options with the user actions you want to be notified about.

Figure 9.10: Email notifications

Creating Zoom Clips

1. From your Zoom client, click the **Clips** icon at the top of your navigation bar.

2. Then, click **New Clip**.

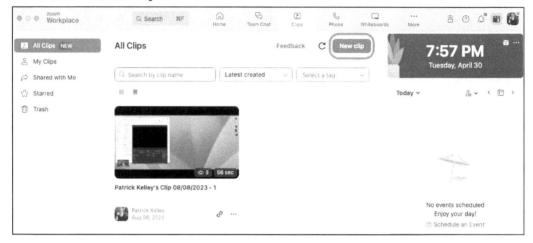

Figure 9.11: New clip

4. A new options window will appear. Choose all the options you want to record, such as screen share, video, or both. Also, your mic, camera, and video resolution are options.

5. **Advanced Settings** also offers options for virtual backgrounds, layouts, and avatars.

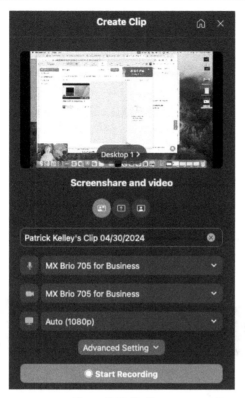

Figure 9.12: Options

6.   Click **Start Recording** once you're ready.

7.   Record your video, share your screen, or demo just like a regular meeting or webinar.

8.   You can annotate, mute, stop video, or even pause with your clips control bar.

9.   Once you are done recording, click **Finish**.

10. A new window will appear with a ton of options. You can add a description or tags. You can also trim and edit the video. You can share with other users as well as copy the link to paste in to use in Zoom Team Chat. You can add call-to-action buttons and customize them. You can even download the .mp4 file should you wish to edit the video with third-party software.

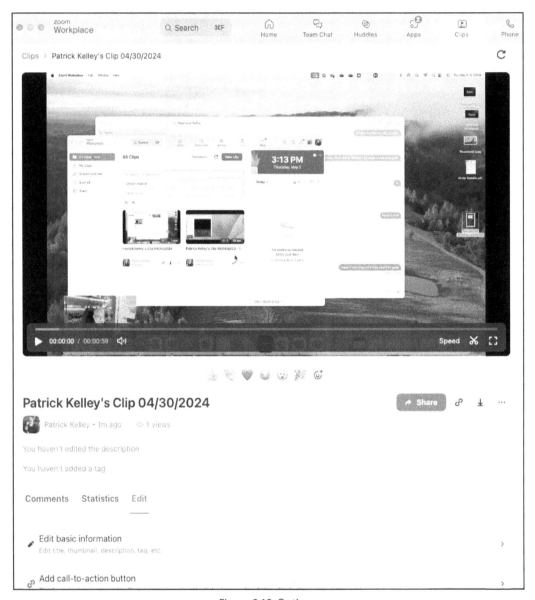

Figure 9.13: Options

11. All the clips that you created and the clips shared with you can easily be accessed from the **Clips** tab at the top of your navigation bar.

12. You can search for past clips or star clips, or even view clips that have been shared with you.

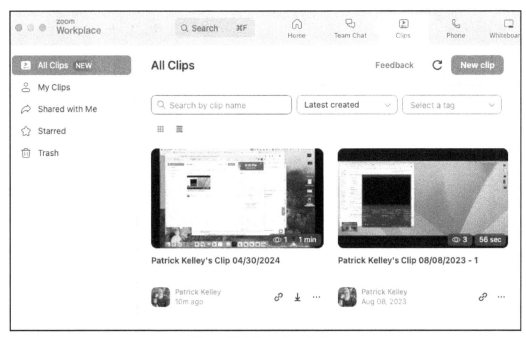

Figure 9.14: Accessing all clips

I hope you've enjoyed learning more about Zoom Clips.

Zoom Huddles

Zoom Huddles are video-enabled virtual coworking spaces designed to create inclusive discussions, bringing fluid interactions of in-person work to remote and hybrid teams throughout the day. Think of them as a water cooler-type feature where workers can have dynamic discussions without the need for a meeting. You can join various Huddles during the day to overhear and contribute to discussion topics without having formal agendas or strict start and stop times. Huddles can be created with unique names, descriptions, and images. Use them as a sort of working area to just hang out during the day when you're not in meetings to brainstorm ideas with colleagues. You can even create fun huddles for social interaction with coworkers. For example, create a huddle called Dog Lovers and join to talk about your dog or share fun pictures.

How to do it...

1. Click the **Huddles** tab in the top navigation bar of your Zoom client.
2. Click the + **New huddle** button.

Figure 9.15: Huddles

3.   Create your huddle. Add a name and description. You can also add a banner and wallpaper to personalize it.

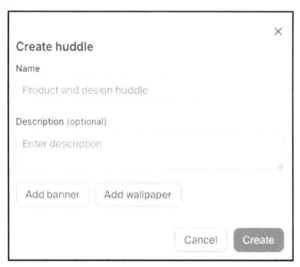

Figure 9.16: Create huddle

4. Your huddle is now active and ready for users to join.

5. You can access the available huddles from Zoom Team Chat. Look for the **Huddle Channels** tab. You can also search for huddles in the search bar of **Team Chat**.

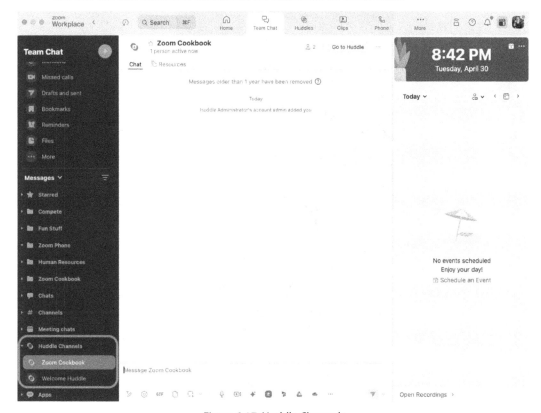

Figure 9.17: Huddle Channels

6. Click the **Go to Huddle** button and you will join the huddle.

7. You can join the huddle with or without your camera on. However, the best practice to increase interaction is to use your camera.

8. A new pop-up huddle window will appear.

Figure 9.18: Huddle window

9. You can now start a conversation with anyone else in the huddle or you can just sit back and listen.

10. Huddles are also chat enabled. You can click the **Team Chat** button and start to contribute to chat conversations in your huddle channel.

11. You can copy the invite link and send it to other people to join as well.

12. You can even play music in the huddle by clicking the **Music** dropdown menu to choose different background music.

13. You'll notice that there is a small control bar to mute your audio and video as well as share content.

14. Click the **More** icon to show even more options.

Figure 9.19: More options

15. If you click the **Music** dropdown button, you can go to your huddle's settings.

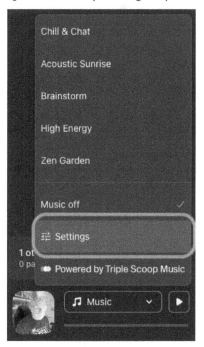

Figure 9.20: Settings

16. A new **Settings** window will open in your Zoom client.

Figure 9.21: The Huddle Settings window

17. Configure your settings to fit your workflow. I have mine set like *Figure 9.18* but choose whatever works best for you.

18. I think you've just become a Zoom Huddles master!

Stream Zoom to social media

I think we can all agree social media has changed the landscape of how we communicate, collaborate, and view content. Platforms such as YouTube, Facebook, and Twitch not only have recorded videos to search and view, but they also allow for live broadcasts, which is also called **streaming**. Live-streaming is the broadcasting of video or audio content in real-time over the internet. Think of TV broadcasts of news or sporting events. These are livestreamed to your TV. The same concept can apply to your next Zoom meeting or webinar. Imagine being able to simply click a button and you could reach an entirely new audience worldwide with Zoom! It's possible and you'll learn how next.

How to do it...

Configure livestreaming in Zoom

1. The first thing you will want to do for higher quality streaming is turn on **Full HD (1080p)**. This isn't a requirement, but it certainly increases the quality of your broadcast.

2. Sign in to your Zoom portal.

3. Click **Account Management**, **Account Settings**, and then click **In Meeting (Advanced)**.

4. Scroll down until you see **Meeting-HD Video Quality** and **Webinar-HD Video Quality**. Toggle these to **Full HD (1080p)**.

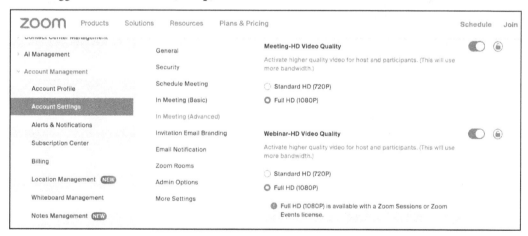

Figure 9.22: HD setting

5. Now, continue scrolling down until you see the **Allow livestreaming** options for meetings and webinars.

Figure 9.23: Live streaming

6. I've toggled on both meetings and webinars. I've also selected all the various platforms as well to give me the option to livestream to any of them if I choose to during my meeting or webinar. (Note that you can only livestream to one platform at a time.)

7. You can enable which platform you use, but for the sake of this recipe, I turned them all on, although I typically only use YouTube.

8. If you or your company have a custom livestreaming service, you can certainly use that too, but that would be outside of the scope of this book. If you want to learn more about that, please visit the whitepaper on that subject here: Custom Live Streaming Service in Zoom (`https://support.zoom.com/hc/en/article?id=zm_kb&sysparm_article=KB0064210`).

9. You're all set to broadcast your next meeting or webinar.

Using live broadcasting

1. Now, in your next Zoom meeting or webinar, you will have a choice for **Live broadcasting**.

2. Click the **More** icon in your control bar, choose **Live broadcasting**, and then pick what platform you want to stream to.

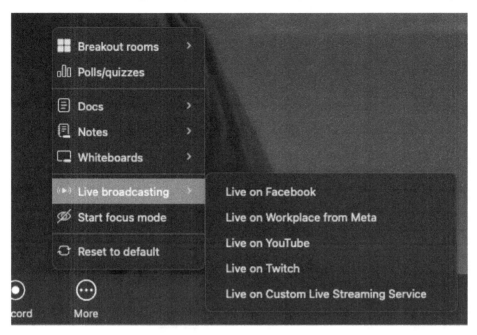

Figure 9.24: Live broadcasting

3. You will, of course, need your own account in the platform you pick. For example, I have a Google account for my Tattooed Nerd YouTube channel (`https://www.youtube.com/c/PatrickKelleyTattooedNerd`), since that is what I stream to normally. When you choose a platform, you will have to log into your account first before you are allowed to stream to that particular service.

4. Once you have authenticated to your platform of choice, you will get a splash screen with options. Typically, these are your meeting title, privacy, and resolution. Each platform varies a little in what information they want to be entered. Here's an example of YouTube.

Figure 9.25: YouTube broadcasting

5. Once you're ready, click **Go Live!**.

6. Now, the platform you picked will start streaming your meeting or webinar live. All your followers on your platform can now view your broadcast from a browser or app, either on their desktop or mobile device.

7. Your followers will see that it is live typically with a **LIVE** notification in the top-left corner of your video. For example, in *Figure 9.23* I am live broadcasting to Facebook.

Figure 9.26: Facebook broadcasting

8. Your audience will be able to interact with you as well with reactions and chats from the platform. You can communicate with your audience by answering questions live during your meeting webinar or chat back with them from the platform you are using to stream.

> **Note**
>
> There is a delay from your real-time Zoom meeting to your platform of choice, which is approximately 5-10 seconds. This is because of nerdy stuff such as compressing your audio and video from Zoom to the platform broadcast service. So, just take that into account when you are interacting with your followers.

9. Once you are done with your live broadcast, just end your Zoom meeting or webinar. This will automatically terminate the live broadcast to your platform.

10. Depending on the platform you used, your live broadcast will now be a video saved in your timeline or channel. Any followers who didn't watch the live broadcast will be able to view the video at any time.

11. That's a wrap on Zoom live broadcasting. Have fun with it!

Using Zoom Apps

You can combine your favorite apps inside Zoom. There's no need to switch from Zoom to your app, as it's probably already embedded in Zoom. For example, do you use Google Drive for all your documents? Zoom has an app for that. Maybe you use *Kahoot!* in your classroom to ask questions – Zoom has that, too. Do you want to present super cool presentations with amazing graphics? Zoom has a Prezi app. What about CRM applications such as Salesforce, Dynamics 365, or HubSpot? Yep, Zoom has that built in as well. Zoom has literally thousands of apps you use every day, which can be integrated into the client. In this recipe, you will learn how to use Zoom Apps to make your workflow more productive. Obviously, we can't dive deep into thousands of apps, but you will learn how to add them to your Zoom client.

How to do it...

1. Sign in to Zoom App Marketplace at `https://marketplace.zoom.us`.

2. You will see thousands of apps you can integrate with Zoom.

3. To get you started, Zoom has created an **Essential Apps** list. This is a list of apps that are very popular and super easy to implement into your workflow.

4. Click the **Essential Apps** tab.

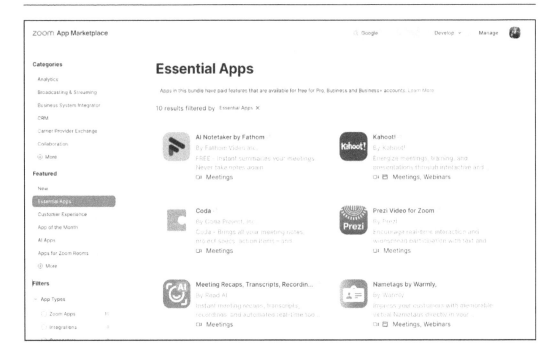

Figure 9.27: Essential Apps

5. Click on any of the apps to add it to your Zoom client or search for any app you might need.

6. As an admin, you need to approve what app can be added for you or your users. Simply toggle the **Approve App** switch to allow you, as well as users in your account, to use the app. For example, in *Figure 9.25*, I have approved the **Kahoot!** app for my users.

Figure 9.28: Kahoot!

7. Now, all users in your account can use the **Kahoot!** app in their next Zoom meeting.

8. This same process can be applied to thousands of apps. Just search Zoom Marketplace for the third-party app you use and Zoom probably has an app that integrates with the client.

9. The next time you or your users have a Zoom meeting, there will be a Zoom Apps icon in the control bar. Click on it to use any approved app.

10. For example, in *Figure 9.26*, I have approved a handful of apps that I think would be helpful for my users.

Figure 9.29: Essential Apps

11. There are apps that integrate with meetings, webinars, and even Team Chat. You can search for apps that integrate with these modalities by filtering your search in Zoom App Marketplace. For example, in *Figure 9.27*, I searched for all Zoom Apps that work with Zoom Team Chat.

Figure 9.30: Team Chat apps

12. One of my favorite apps is Google Drive for Team Chat. Click on **Google Drive** to add it to your Zoom client. When you click on any app, a new browser window will appear to approve the app for yourself as well as add it to other users if you're the admin.

Figure 9.31: Google Drive

13. For example, I am a Zoom admin for my company and can add any app for any user. If I wanted to add Google Drive for every user, I would click the **Add for Others** button from *Figure 9.28* and a new window would appear.

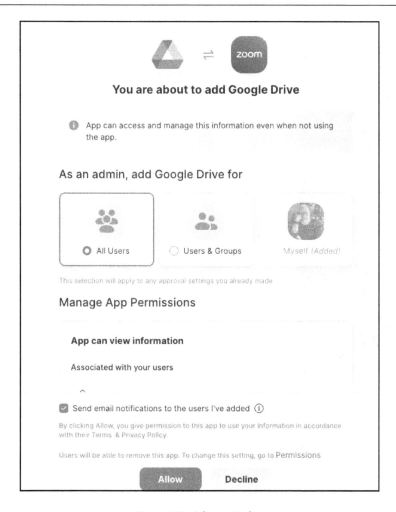

Figure 9.32: Admin window

14. I chose **All Users**, but you can pick specific users or groups as well.

15. Now, to approve the app, click **Allow**. You can also choose to alert users via email that you have approved a new app for them to use.

16. Since Google Drive is a Team Chat app, I can start using it from Zoom Team Chat.

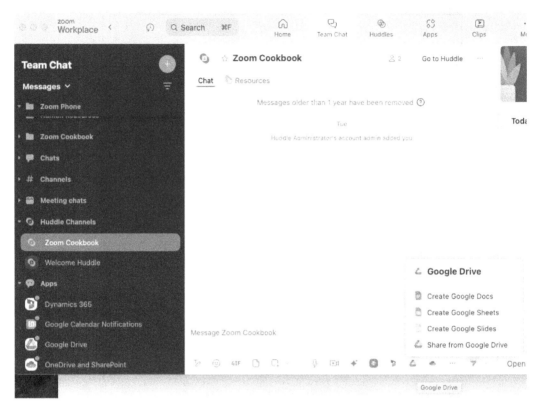

Figure 9.33: Google Drive

17. In the Team Chat message creation window, you can now see that I have a Google Drive app. I can now create and share Google Docs, Sheets, and Slides directly from the Zoom client. This is the app I probably use most often. I no longer need to go to a separate browser to create Google documents; I can do it directly from the Zoom client. I think that is super cool.

18. But you are probably asking yourself, "But what if I use OneDrive?" Don't worry, Zoom has an app for that, too! Just add OneDrive from Zoom App Marketplace. It's a Team Chat app too and works the same way that the Google Drive app works, allowing you to create and share Office 365 documents from Team Chat.

Figure 9.34: OneDrive

19. You'll also notice that there is an **Apps** tab in the top navigation bar of your Zoom client. Click on it to manage the apps you already have and even add new ones; you don't always have to do it from Zoom App Marketplace. Zoom makes it pretty easy.

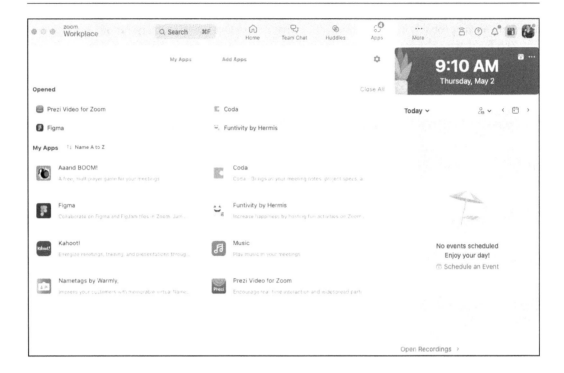

Figure 9.35: Zoom Apps

20. Not all apps are for your business workflows and integrations. There are even interactive games you can play with your attendees. For example, try *Funtivity* or *Heads Up!*.

21. It's impossible to dive into every app that Zoom supports as there are literally thousands. I just wanted to show you some of the possibilities within Zoom on how to enable Zoom Apps.

22. Feel free to explore all the apps in Zoom App Marketplace and see how they can help improve your productivity. Imagine using all the third-party apps you use every day inside of Zoom!

Using avatars and filters

Not every Zoom call is a serious business meeting. A lot of times, Zoom meetings are with friends or family. Even meetings with co-workers or colleagues need to be fun and engaging. Zoom can help add levity to your interactions with filters, for example. You can apply filters to your real-time video in meetings and webinars. They are meant to be a funny way to interact with your meeting attendees. You can wear virtual sunglasses or hats, or maybe you want some bunny ears. They even have facial recognition, so they are dynamic and move with your head and eyes to always stay where they are supposed to. Zoom already has a bunch installed in your client, but you can even customize your own if you want.

Zoom avatars are another great option when you want to add some levity to a meeting. Perhaps you aren't feeling completely camera ready but still want to engage with your audience with a custom avatar. Avatars can help you express yourself even without a live video but can still show your emotions and body language, such as smiling or nodding. The avatar will literally mirror your head movements and facial expressions from your video feed.

So, let's dive into the recipes to learn more.

How to do it...

Filters

1. Go to **Settings** in your Zoom client, click the **Background & effects** tab, and then choose **Video filters**.

2. You will see a number of filters that can be added to your real-time Zoom video. Just click on any of them to see a preview of what your attendees will see. Wear sunglasses, wear a hat, or even frame your entire video. I'm a pirate!

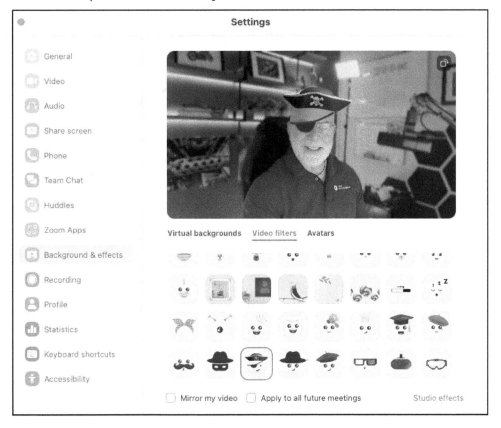

Figure 9.36: Filters

3. You can also add custom filters that you design yourself.

4. You can apply effects by clicking the **Studio effects** link at the bottom right.

5. With **Studio effects**, you can apply effects such as different eyebrows, facial hair, or even lip color.

6. Have fun with **Video filters** in your next meeting everyone will be asking, "How did you do that?"

Avatars

1. Click the **Avatars** tab next to **Video filters**.

2. Zoom has several animal avatars that you can use. Just click one and it will apply to your video feed.

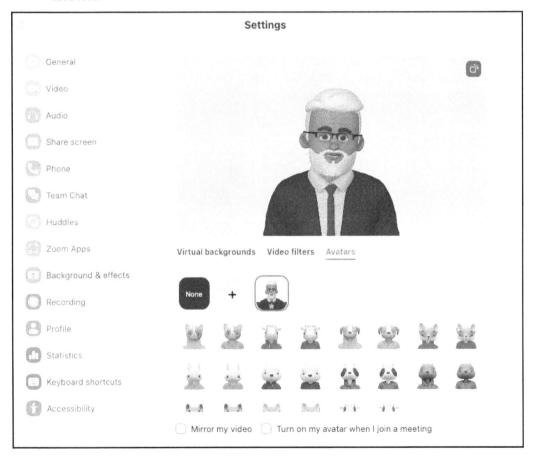

Figure 9.37: Avatars

3. My personal favorite is to design my own avatar to look like myself. Click the + icon to get started.

4. A new avatar design window will open. You can see that there are a ton of options to customize your own avatar, such as hair, eyes, and even beards. Get creative and have fun!

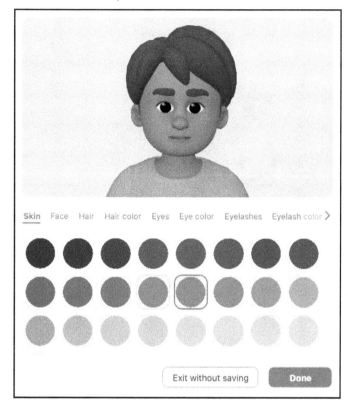

Figure 9.38: Custom avatar

5. You can actually design multiple avatars to use during your next meeting. Design as many as you want, depending on your mood!

6. Now, to use your avatar, join or start a new Zoom meeting.

7. Click on the **Video ^** icon, choose **Choose avatar…**, and pick the avatar you designed or any of the default Zoom ones.

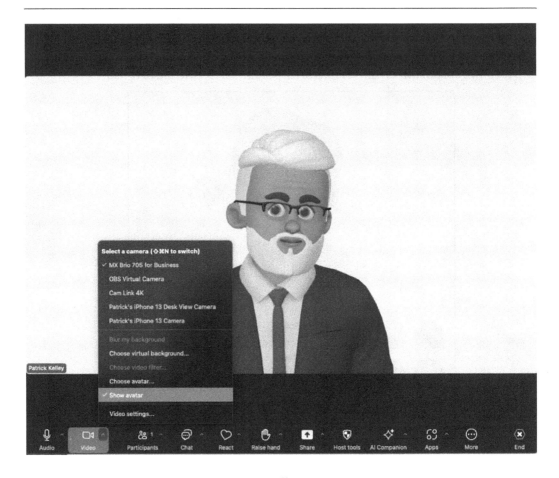

Figure 9.39: Show avatar

8. A best practice is to leave your camera on so your avatar shows your emotions and head and face movements. Try it! Smile. Nod. Raise your eyebrows. They all work with your avatar. If you mute your camera, just your avatar is shown with no emotions or facial tracking, which is boring.

9. Pretty cool, right? Have fun with filters and avatars!

Using a secondary camera

There might be some use cases where you will need to show a physical item, such as a prototype, piece of paper, or even a physical whiteboard. For these types of situations, you would require two cameras. One, obviously, shows you as a presenter, but a second camera can show the item you wish to share in the meeting. Zoom can handle this workflow easily.

How to do it...

1. Start or join any Zoom meeting.

2. Click **Share** from the control bar then click the **Advanced** tab.

3. You will see a **Second camera** option to share a second camera; choose it and then click the **Share** button. (Remember the *Layouts* recipe? It still applies here.)

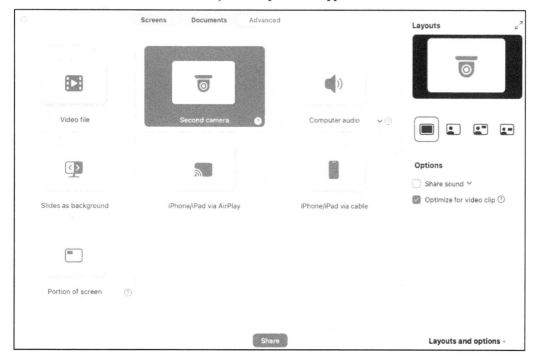

Figure 9.40: Second camera

4. Now, your second camera will be shared during the meeting as well as the camera you are using to present.

5. The meeting attendees will now see your second camera feed enlarged just as if you were sharing a document or whiteboard. Now, you can demo your product, gadget, or super cool fidget spinner!

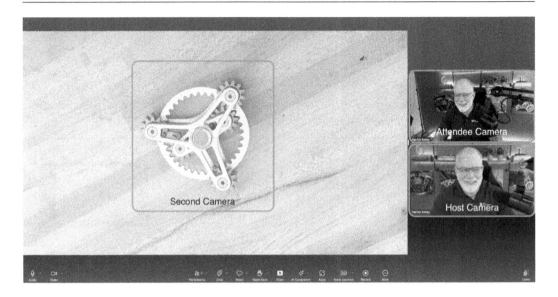

Figure 9.41: Second camera

6.   I've seen teachers use a second camera to demonstrate a science project or write out math questions on a piece of paper. I've even seen users point a second camera at a whiteboard to draw out architectural designs.

7.   Come up with your own unique use case for using a second camera!

Enhancing video quality

Zoom is known for video conferences, therefore, you want to maximize your video quality as much as possible with some settings within the Zoom client. These simple settings can make a big difference in your next meeting.

How to do it...

1.   Go to the **Settings** window of your Zoom client and click the **Video** tab.

2.   You'll see your **Camera** settings.

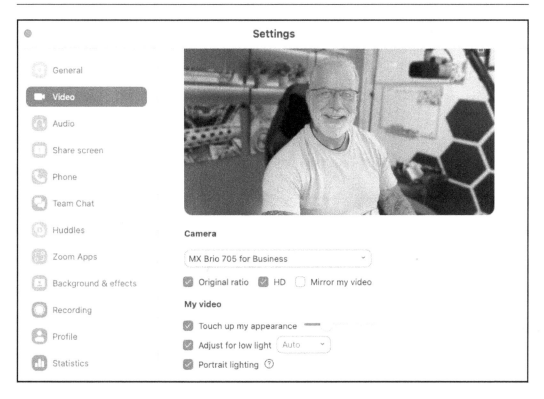

Figure 9.42: The Video settings

3. Make sure **HD** is checked for HD video. This requires approximately 2-3 Mbps of bandwidth to work.

4. Toggle the **Touch up my appearance** option. This makes your video appear softer and smoother, enhancing your appearance in real time. It smooths blemishes on your skin as well. You can adjust the level of touch up by using the slide bar.

5. If you don't have any dedicated lighting or you're in a low-light environment, you can brighten your video by checking **Adjust for low light**. By default, it is set to **Auto** and Zoom adjusts this for you, but you can choose **Manual** and adjust it yourself.

6. **Portrait lighting** is my favorite hidden gem for improving quality. This feature highlights you and then dims your background to bring more attention and focus to your face and body for your attendees. Try it.

OK, that is all the settings to improve video in your client. Experiment with them.

Improving audio quality

Having great audio is actually the most important item you can have to have a great meeting experience. I would say it's more important than high-quality video. Being able to articulate your message with clear and precise audio is the number one thing you need using Zoom. It makes a big difference.

How to do it...

1. Go to **Settings** in your Zoom client, click the **Audio** tab, and then navigate to the **Microphone** section.

Figure 9.43: Audio settings

2. Check the **Automatically adjust microphone volume** setting. This allows Zoom to adjust the volume gain on your microphone for optimum sound volume for your attendees.

3. Next, navigate to the **Audio profile** section.

    By default, **Zoom background noise removal** is set to **Auto**. This is the option recommended for most situations. This allows Zoom to use software audio processing to give the highest quality sound for most users. You can manually set this to low, medium, or high depending on your environment.

4. **Personalized audio isolation** is recommended when you are in crowded places such as airports or restaurants.

5. Zoom will capture and analyze a voiceprint from your meeting audio then enhance your voice clarity and remove background noise. You can even record a voiceprint to further improve performance.

6. Once you click on **Personalized audio isolation**, a notification will appear, asking your permission to use your voice. Click **OK** to proceed.

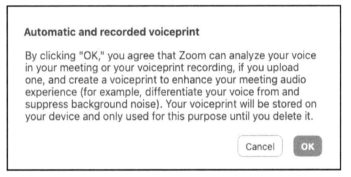

Figure 9.44: Voiceprint

7. Now, you have the option to create a voiceprint recording. I would recommend you create one for greater performance in loud environments such as when you are in an airport or restaurant with a lot of noise. Zoom will then use your voiceprint to filter out background noises.

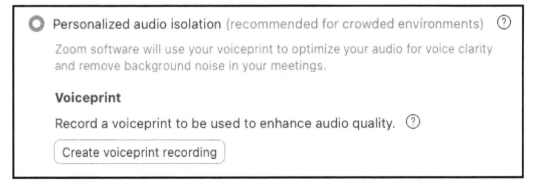

Figure 9.45: Create voiceprint

8. Click **Create voiceprint recording** and a new window will appear.

9. You can now follow the directions and start recording.

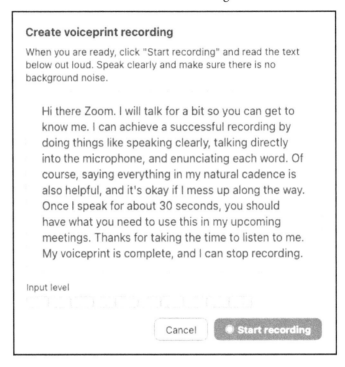

Figure 9.46: Record voiceprint

10. Once you have stopped recording, Zoom will now use your voiceprint to optimize audio input.

11. This audio file will now be stored on your computer. You can update the voiceprint at any time. You can also delete it altogether:

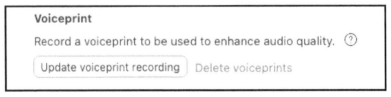

Figure 9.47: Voiceprint

12. If you're a musician, this next setting, **Original sound for musicians**, is for you.

Figure 9.48: Audio profile

13. There are three options available to choose from inside this profile:

- **High-fidelity music mode**: This optimizes Zoom audio for the highest quality music. This disables echo cancellation and post-processing. It raises the audio codec quality to 48Khz @ 96Kpbs-mono/192Kbps-stereo. This also increases CPU consumption and requires greater bandwidth. It's recommended that your computer be plugged into an Ethernet cable and not using Wi-Fi. A professional audio interface, microphone, and studio headphones are required.

- **Echo cancellation**: This prevents echoes from being captured or created between your microphone and speakers to improve audio quality. Unless you are using headphones or playing an instrument, I recommend you enable this option.

- **Stereo audio**: This option enables Zoom to encode audio into stereo. A stereo-capable microphone or audio interface is required. This does increase CPU utilization and consumes more bandwidth.

14. The last option available is **Live performance audio**.

Use this when playing live music during a meeting with other musicians. Obviously, when performing, you need to have your timing and harmony in sync with the other musicians to play a great song. This option's goal is to reduce the audio latency between all participants to approximately 30-50ms.

15. All the musicians in the meeting must also have this toggled on to utilize this feature.

Well, I think that about sums up how to improve your audio! Good luck!

Appendix A

Zoom has consistently been evaluated in studies as having the highest quality video of any meeting or conferencing platform. I won't bore you with the nerdy stuff of why, such as diving deep into QoS, latency, jitter, resolution, and so on. Just know that Zoom consistently wins for not the best video quality and is a great start for having high-quality video and audio.

But in this *Appendix* chapter, I want to dive into how you can improve the overall quality of your next Zoom meeting. It's a multilayered approach with many factors that contribute. For example, there are some simple features you can configure in your client to improve audio and video quality, but there are also some advanced hardware configurations that you can implement to make Zoom professional-grade. All these features work synergistically together. The more features and hardware you implement, the higher the quality of your video and audio.

I would guess that almost every single laptop or PC you buy today probably has a camera, microphone, and speaker installed. I can tell you from experience those are by far the lowest quality level you can use in Zoom. Do they work? Of course. Do they work well? Maybe. Can you get top-notch and amazing high-quality Zoom audio and video? No. But maybe having super high-quality video and audio isn't that important to you, and that is totally fine. For example, you might use Zoom to have simple meetings with friends and family, and you just want to quickly open your laptop and have a quick video call, and that is great. Regardless of your workflow, this chapter can make your Zoom quality better.

In this *Appendix* section, we're going to cover the following topics:

- Examining camera performance
- Understanding microphones
- Exploring lighting essentials

The following three sections in this chapter don't really follow the same format as you're used to in this cookbook.

They are more informative without specific How to do it… guides. So, let's dive in.

Examining camera performance

There are three kinds of cameras generally available. First are simple cameras built into your laptop; second, a quality webcam that you can plug into your computer via a USB cable; and third, a super high-quality DSLR camera at a professional level.

Probably every laptop you can buy today has a camera built in, and the quality is what you might expect. It gets the job done for basic meetings, but it's not crystal clear. It probably isn't 1080p. The autofocus is subpar, and the facial tracking features are probably non-existent. This would be OK for simple Zoom meetings but is the lowest-level quality of the three choices.

At a minimum, I would recommend you invest in a quality USB webcam. For around $150, you could easily upgrade the overall quality of your video exponentially. For example, I use a webcam that has a full 4K, with great auto-focus and facial recognition tracking, that I bought on Amazon for $199. It's the Logitech MX Brio 705. It's fantastic, and Logitech isn't paying me to say that! It also comes with free software that allows you to fully customize your camera settings such as exposure, lighting, contrast, and saturation. Of course, there are a ton of options in this space. Companies such as Jabra, HP, and even Microsoft make good-quality cameras. USB webcams are far higher quality than a laptop camera and are completely worth their cost. You don't even need a 4K camera if you are on a budget. A good-quality 1080p camera will run you around $50.

If you want to upgrade to the highest possible level of quality, go for a DSLR camera like the professionals use for pictures and videos. These, of course, are more expensive, ranging from $500 to thousands of dollars. These allow for amazing video quality with interchangeable lenses for every situation. These typically connect via an HDMI or USB-C cable to your PC or Mac for 1080p quality. But you can also use a hardware interface such as the Elgato Cam Link 4K to upgrade to 4K with a USB 3.0 port.

The quality of video you need should dictate what camera to use. For example, I produce a ton of video content and I am in Zoom meetings all day long, so it was worth it for me to upgrade to a DSLR camera. And yes, I have the most amazing quality video typically in every Zoom meeting. But you can get great video quality with a good USB webcam, plus they are portable. You can throw it in your backpack with your laptop when you are on the go. There are a lot of YouTube channels out there that dive deep into all sorts of camera gear. One of my favorites is *Senpai Gaming*. Visit this link if you want to learn more: `https://www.youtube.com/Senpai.`

Hope you learned something about cameras!

Understanding microphones

What's the most important part of a quality meeting or webinar? What if I told you it's actually great audio? Let's learn more about producing great-sounding webinars.

Just as with video, every laptop comes with a microphone. Guess what? It's probably not great, although the brand-new Apple MacBooks are actually pretty good. Good audio is crucial to keep attendee engagement. While video certainly helps make Zoom meetings more personal and engaging, clear-quality audio is more essential. You could literally have your camera off and still have an excellent meeting with great content and great audio.

The first thing you need to do is have a good (if not great) microphone that isn't from your laptop. Upgrading to a quality webcam is one option. The built-in microphone on modern webcams is way better than what's built into your laptop. A lot of modern webcams even have dual microphones with beamforming. That's sort of a fancy way to enhance sound quality and reduce environmental noise.

Some people prefer a quality headset. These have a built-in mic that is close to your mouth, providing optimal audio quality. Headsets also typically have built-in noise reduction software that cancels out background noise. Plus, they are comfortable to wear, but sometimes during your meetings, you may want a more professional look, so maybe headsets aren't for you.

Probably the best and least expensive option is a dedicated USB microphone that plugs directly into your computer. You can get a great USB mic for around $50. They are simple to set up and use right out of the box, with no additional software or hardware needed. They usually have professional-level audio quality. A lot of podcasters, streamers, and content creators use USB microphones. This is an ideal way to get great-quality audio during a Zoom meeting at an affordable price. One of my favorites is the Maono AU-A04. The last time I looked, it was around $55 on Amazon: `https://a.co/d/gOtiW8G`.

Last is an XLR-type microphone. This is what the professional recording industry uses. As you can imagine, this takes a lot more money and some decent technical knowledge to set up. It also requires extra hardware such as an audio interface to connect to your computer. I actually use an XLR dynamic for all my Zoom events. Is this required for great audio in a meeting? No, but it is the best-sounding audio you can have.

So, you have a lot of choices in microphones, obviously. At a minimum, I would recommend upgrading to a USB microphone for the best audio quality at an affordable price.

Exploring lighting essentials

What's the number one way to get great video quality? By the way, the answer isn't a great camera. It's actually lighting.

For example, in *Figure A1.1*, I'm using just the room lights in my office:

Figure A1.1: Room lights

Just by adding one light to the mix, we can vastly improve video quality, as you can see in *Figure A1.2*:

Figure A1.2: Adding one light to the mix

Now, what about multiple lights? Even better results, as you can see from *Figure A1.3*:

Figure A1.3: Adding multiple lights

I think you get the idea: lighting makes a huge difference.

Having good lighting is the best way to get a great-quality Zoom video. This could be as simple as sitting by a window for natural light or as complex as a completely professional lit stage. Let's start simple and go complex.

If you have access to move your laptop and camera next to a softly lit natural light room, then take advantage. It's free. Just make sure no shadows are going across your face.

Next is a simple LED or ring light. You can get these easily for $20. They work OK, but you get what you pay for. Make sure it has a light diffuser on it, though. Harsh LEDs aren't very complimentary to skin tones on camera. You typically place these in front of you, but play with the angles. For example, put it 20 to 45 degrees left or right to create some cool shadows on your face. Also, place it high, aiming down in case you wear glasses to get rid of reflections.

Two-point lighting systems are even better. The main light is a good-quality diffused LED light called a key light. This is your main light source and should be placed around 45 degrees from where you sit. The second light is called a fill light, and this goes on the other side to reduce shadows from the key light. Play with the angles for the best results. Make sure both are high, and aim down to reduce glare on glasses:

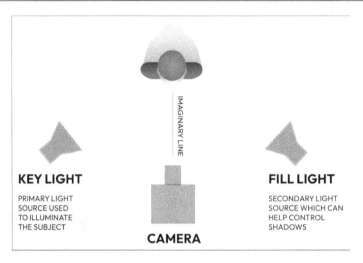

Figure A1.4: Two-point lighting

The optimal lighting system is called three-point lighting. You have your key light and fill lights, but you also have what they call a back light, sometimes called a hair light. This goes behind you directly opposite your fill light. This helps separate you from the background, creating depth. I have mine above me and at 45 degrees to give me good light around my hair and shoulders:

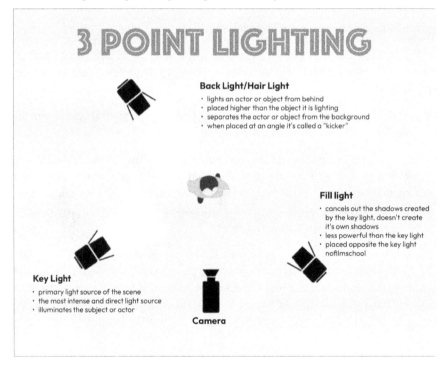

Figure A1.5: Three-point lighting

Each of my lights is also set at 5200k. This is what they call light temperature. 5200k is a good balance of warmth and coolness to closely match natural lights. You'll also want to match your camera's white balance to your lighting to give you the best skin tones. I encourage you to experiment with angles, lighting, and white balance. It'll take a bit of practice to get it right, but it will make a world of difference in your next Zoom meeting. Search on YouTube for a lot of instructional videos on how to properly set up lighting.

Also, I have what I call motivational or ambience lighting behind me too. See along my shelves. These are RGB lights that allow me to give even more depth and character to my videos. Keep these subtle, but they make a pretty distinct difference in creating a warm and inviting look for your video. You can even change the colors to match your brand or even add seasonal or holiday themes:

Figure A1.6: RGB lights

I love talking about lighting. It makes such a huge difference.

Appendix B

After you have successfully logged into Zoom, your client will appear. Let's spend the rest of the time in this Appendix familiarizing you with some of the functions of the Zoom client. This will be more of a high-level overview as many of the functions have been discussed in depth in the cookbook.

Home Screen

When you launch the Zoom client the first page displayed is the Home Screen:

Figure A2.1: Home Screen

This screen has 5 major functions:

1. **New Meeting** – This creates a new Ad Hoc meeting with no participants other than yourself. Ad Hoc meetings are impromptu meetings that haven't been scheduled, such as when a user wants to discuss something with another user via a quick unplanned meeting. You can invite additional attendees after the meeting has started.

2. **Join** – This button joins an already established meeting. You will need to know the Zoom Meeting ID to use this function. This will have either been shared with you in a chat or email previously.

3. **Schedule** – This schedules a future Zoom meeting allowing you as the meeting organizer to invite attendees and configure the meeting with things like Waiting Rooms, Meeting Recordings, and Chat.

4. **Share Screen** – This function allows you to share your computer screen in two different ways.

5. Share your screen to a Zoom Room with a Sharing Key.

6. Share your screen to a Zoom meeting with a Meeting ID.

7. **Calendar** – On the right side of the Home Screen you will see your Calendar. This will have your meetings for you and allow you to join them with a simple click.

Top Navigation Bar

Located at the top of the Zoom client in your Top Navigation Bar, this is how you will toggle between all the functions within Zoom. Think of these as shortcuts to get to the different collaboration and communication features of Zoom. Let's do a quick review of what all these buttons and icons do. To dive deeper into the exact use of each of these areas please see the corresponding recipes, but for now, let's become familiar with the design and layout of your Zoom client.

Figure A2.2: Top Navigation Bar

Starting from left to right, we will describe each function and its use.

Arrows

The arrows are backward and forward controls that are only used in the Team Chat function (Team Chat will be covered fully in *Chapter 5*). These allow you to quickly go back and forth between various chat conversations that you've had using Team Chat. This is a quick way for you to toggle between chat conversations with either individuals or group chats. We will dive deeper into Team Chat in a later recipe.

Figure A2.3: Team Chat Arrows

History

These are the last 10 conversations you've had in Team Chat. You can click the History icon and quickly navigate to any of those conversations and click on the one you want. This feature is only used in Team Chat.

Figure A2.4: Conversation History

Search

This function allows you to quickly search for items such as Contacts, Team Chat Channels, Team Chat Messages, and Files. The results are displayed in your Search menu. Also, any past searches are also displayed should you want just to utilize them instead of entering your search criteria again. From the displayed results you can quickly click on them and jump to the appropriate result.

Figure A2.5: Search

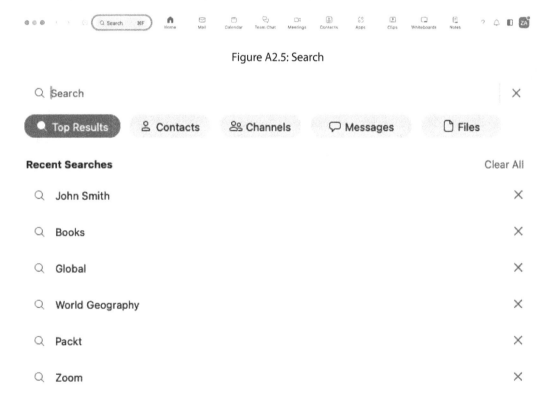

Figure A2.6: Search Results

Home

This icon takes you back to the original Home Screen we discussed earlier.

Figure A2.7: Home Screen Icon

Mail

Your Zoom client can also be your email client and should utilize either Google, Microsoft or even Zoom as your email provider. You can quickly navigate to all your emails right from Zoom without having to go to a separate email client such as Gmail or Outlook. Everything like reading, replying, and forwarding emails can be done directly from your Zoom client saving you time and not having to switch clients.

Figure A2.8: Mail Client

Calendar

You can configure your Zoom client to also be your Calendar client with providers such as Google, Microsoft, or Zoom. You can quickly navigate to your Calendar directly from your Zoom client without having to go to a separate calendar client like Google Calendar or Outlook. This will save you a lot of time no longer having to toggle between separate clients. Everything can be done directly from Zoom!

Figure A2.9: Calendar Client

Team Chat

This is probably one of your most valuable tools and we will dive much deeper into Team Chat in *Chapter 5*. But to quickly navigate to all your 1:1 and channel chats you can click on the Team Chat icon in the navigation bar.

Figure A2.10: Team Chat

Meetings

This is the cornerstone of Zoom – Meetings! Clicking on this icon will take you to all your previously scheduled meetings for today and tomorrow. You can also start and schedule meetings. You will be able to view your entire calendar as well as watch any previously recorded meetings.

Figure A2.11: Zoom Meetings

Contacts

You can quickly go to all your Zoom Contacts from this icon. In the Contacts area, you will be able to collaborate and communicate with individual contacts. You can efficiently be able to start any number of modalities with one click such as Call, Meet, and Chat with contacts. If you have Zoom Phone, you will also be able to SMS to text individuals. All your Contacts' personal information will be easily available from here as well. Things like location, phone numbers, and email.

Figure A2.12: Zoom Contacts

Zoom Apps

Zoom Apps allow seamless integration of third party applications in both the Zoom Client and Zoom Meetings. They are designed to improve collaboration, engage your team, or build customer relationships. Zoom Apps allows applications to work alongside you in the Zoom ecosystem. An example might be to use a timer in a Zoom meeting to keep speakers on track or play music during a Zoom meeting. There are over 2500 apps to use in Zoom currently. Imagine being able to launch apps inside of a meeting instead of sharing your screen separately. Zoom Apps create a more immersive and effective experience for users inside of Zoom Meetings or out. We will be diving into Zoom Apps more in a separate chapter.

Figure A2.13: Zoom Apps

Zoom Clips

Zoom Clips allows you to easily record, edit, and share high-quality video messages. These short-form video messages can be shared internally or externally with users, contacts, and even groups. Sometimes it's easier to record a video describing an event, or project or share your screen than have a separate meeting. With Zoom Clips users can now communicate asynchronously and still deliver concise and precise video presentations. This will assist presenters and attendees in cutting down on meetings and calls and even help reduce lost productivity by delivering precise messaging in an effective and easy-to-deliver manner.

Figure A2.14: Zoom Clips

Whiteboards

Zoom designed its whiteboard to be a place where users can brainstorm, create, collaborate, and co-author on a persistent, expandable, and digital canvas. Whiteboards can be used to draw, ideate, share, and present from any Zoom client or device. By clicking this icon, you will be taken to all the whiteboards you've created as well as all whiteboards that have been shared with you from other users. You can create new Projects and create new whiteboards here too.

Figure A2.15: Whiteboards

Notes

Notes is a Zoom workspace used to create and collaborate during the entire meeting lifecycle. There are 3 lifecycles Before, During, and After. Notes allow users to not only create meeting notes but also share those notes with other meeting participants. Since Notes is a collaboration document all meeting participants can both view the notes as well as contribute. Clicking Notes will take you to the Zoom Notes area where you can view recent notes as well as notes that have been shared with you by others.

Help Center

When you have questions about Zoom the first place to look is the Zoom Help Center. This website is full of valuable information that can probably answer almost any question you have about Zoom. There are getting-started guides, troubleshooting steps, learning centers, and a full Zoom community to find solutions and ask questions. Next time you have a question about anything Zoom try here first!

Figure A2.16: Zoom Help Center

Activity Center

All your recent Zoom notifications can be found here in the Activity Center. You can view these in this area. Notifications are defined as cloud recordings, missed phone and video calls, received voicemails, SMS messages, and whiteboards. When a new activity appears, a red alert will be displayed above the bell notifying you of new activity in Zoom.

Figure A2.17: Zoom Activity Center

Calendar Panel

You can choose to have a separate calendar panel always open by clicking this icon. Enabling this feature creates a panel on the right side of the Zoom client that is pinned, therefore all your meetings for the day are immediately accessible from any Zoom application. This can save you time with context switching. Allowing you as a user to see immediately your entire Zoom Meetings schedule for the day. You can also join any meeting with one click directly from the Calendar Panel. Should you want the screen real estate back, for example you are designing a big whiteboard, you can simply click the Calendar Panel icon again and it will toggle the right panel away.

Figure A2.18: Zoom Calendar Panel

Index

Z

packtpub.com

Subscribe to our online digital library for full access to over 7,000 books and videos, as well as industry leading tools to help you plan your personal development and advance your career. For more information, please visit our website.

Why subscribe?

- Spend less time learning and more time coding with practical eBooks and Videos from over 4,000 industry professionals

- Improve your learning with Skill Plans built especially for you

- Get a free eBook or video every month

- Fully searchable for easy access to vital information

- Copy and paste, print, and bookmark content

Did you know that Packt offers eBook versions of every book published, with PDF and ePub files available? You can upgrade to the eBook version at packtpub.com and as a print book customer, you are entitled to a discount on the eBook copy. Get in touch with us at customercare@packtpub.com for more details.

At www.packtpub.com, you can also read a collection of free technical articles, sign up for a range of free newsletters, and receive exclusive discounts and offers on Packt books and eBooks.

Other Books You May Enjoy

If you enjoyed this book, you may be interested in these other books by Packt:

Supercharging Productivity with Trello

Brittany Joiner

ISBN: 978-1-80181-387-7

- Explore Trello's structure and the important features
- Customize Trello cards and fields to fit your use case
- Create Trello views to get a mile-high view of your projects
- Discover Trello's automation features to save time and automate tasks
- Use Power-Ups for documentation, reporting, contacts, and more
- Get the most out of Trello with real-world examples and practical tips

Supercharge your Slack Productivity

Moshe Markovich

ISBN: 978-1-80056-962-1

- Understand how to set up a Slack workspace
- Migrate existing workspaces to your organization
- Explore expert tips and techniques for using Slack effectively
- Improve collaboration within your team by integrating multiple apps with Slack
- Find the right bots and apps to use for your workspace
- Discover how to build your own Slack bot
- Explore the right channels on Slack to improve your presence in professional communities
- Find the best solutions for automating your work directly through Slack

Packt is searching for authors like you

If you're interested in becoming an author for Packt, please visit `authors.packtpub.com` and apply today. We have worked with thousands of developers and tech professionals, just like you, to help them share their insight with the global tech community. You can make a general application, apply for a specific hot topic that we are recruiting an author for, or submit your own idea.

Share Your Thoughts

Now you've finished *The Ultimate Zoom Cookbook*, we'd love to hear your thoughts! Scan the QR code below to go straight to the Amazon review page for this book and share your feedback or leave a review on the site that you purchased it from.

https://packt.link/r/1804616990

Your review is important to us and the tech community and will help us make sure we're delivering excellent quality content.

Download a free PDF copy of this book

Thanks for purchasing this book!

Do you like to read on the go but are unable to carry your print books everywhere?

Is your eBook purchase not compatible with the device of your choice?

Don't worry, now with every Packt book you get a DRM-free PDF version of that book at no cost.

Read anywhere, any place, on any device. Search, copy, and paste code from your favorite technical books directly into your application.

The perks don't stop there, you can get exclusive access to discounts, newsletters, and great free content in your inbox daily

Follow these simple steps to get the benefits:

1. Scan the QR code or visit the link below

https://packt.link/free-ebook/9781804616994

2. Submit your proof of purchase
3. That's it! We'll send your free PDF and other benefits to your email directly

www.ingramcontent.com/pod-product-compliance
Lightning Source LLC
Chambersburg PA
CBHW080621060326
40690CB00021B/4770